Breathe

A COURSE of MEDITATION and REFLECTION

Bryan Meadows

Breathe: A Course in Meditation and Reflection
Bryan Meadows

©2020, Bryan Meadows
www.bryanmeadows.com
bryan@embassychurchatl.com

Published by Embassy Advantage™

Cover Design by Jason Long

Editing Team:
Tiffany Buckner
Vanessa Hunter
Glenda Giles

Research Team:
Tiffany Buckner

ISBN: 978-1-7348612-3-5

Table of Contents

Introduction

In the 60's, a new movement started called the New Age Movement. It originated in occultic and metaphysical communities, and it started to gain momentum in the 70's and 80's. Proponents for this movement began to embrace what the church had long rejected—science! Not only did they embrace science, but they also embraced a lot of religious views (Christian, Hindu and pagan), including the arts of meditation and reflection. Consequently, the church began to distance herself from any and everything that the New Age Movement (and every other occultic trend) embraced. In other words, the church grew more and more passive, while the occult grew more and more assertive. But the problem with this is—meditation is actually a Christian practice, and so is reflection! And since then, the church has sat on the sidelines and watched helplessly as many occultists claimed and renamed our beliefs and our systems as their own, and any time this happens, the church takes another step back while Satan takes another step forward. In other words, we've been losing ground, but not anymore!

Breathe is a unique and ground-breaking guide that deals with the art of Christian meditation and reflection. In this informative and eye-opening masterpiece, you will learn about the origin and nature of the very breath you breathe and how to make it work for you! You will learn effective breathing techniques that will help you overcome worry, anxiety, fear, depression and every other issue that arises in your mind! And hear me—this is more than a book, it is an extensive course and a movement! The history and the revelation packed in this book will help you to understand why Satan fears meditation!

Every chapter in this book is bursting with information!
After you've finished reading a chapter, you will find:

Meditation Moment	Here, you will find a book of the Bible listed. Your assignment is to list the text in the space provided using the MPS™ (see next chapter).
Word Study	Here, you will take keywords that you've extracted from the Meditation Moment, and conduct a word study.
Let's Reflect	In this space, you will reflect on what you've learned in the scriptures and from the chapter you've just read.
My Alarm Clock	In this section, you will learn little known facts about how your body responds to sleep and how meditation helps to give you a better night's rest. Additionally, you will be able to record and track how meditation is improving your sleep regime.

Simply follow the directions after each chapter.

Implementation

There are many ways to meditate that don't necessarily involve what we commonly see the world doing. Whenever you're meditating on a scripture, a good practice is to inhale and hold your breath for five to ten seconds. This gives you time to focus on what you've read. You can also:

1. **Read a scripture repeatedly.** The goal is to commit it to memory. As you learn it by heart, you would then recite it from your memory. This allows the scripture to travel from the surface of your heart (short term memory) to the center of your heart (long term memory).

2. **Incorporate what you've studied in your prayers.** For example, if you've studied Psalms 23:1, you could pray, "Lord, you are my Shepherd. I shall not want." This is called reflection.

3. **Incorporate what you've studied in your worship.** When you're singing songs of praise to the Lord or simply worshiping Him, you can reflect on what you've learned about Him by incorporating it in your worship.

4. **Make it personal.** Psalm 34:18 reads, "The LORD is nigh unto them that are of a broken heart; and saveth such as be of a contrite spirit." If you're dealing with a broken heart, you could meditate on this scripture in a way that makes it personal to you. For example, you'd say, "The Lord is near them who have a broken heart. The Lord is near

me."

5. **Use sticky notes:** Write down what you've studied on a sticky note and post it up all around your house. Every time you see the sticky note, stop to meditate and/or reflect on that particular scripture.

Meditation Point System

The Meditation Point System (MPS) is a system I've developed to help believers to get the most out of meditation. Please note that secular movements that promote meditation have their own systems, and they use what they call "points" in a different way. In short, their points are just tidbits of information or we can say bullet points. However, the system I've developed involves a simple process of breaking down the scriptures in a way that would allow you to remember them.

The MPS™ works this way. You read (or list) a scripture that you want to meditate on. From there, using the space below (or a separate notebook), list each line in a way that stands out to you. For example, look at the scripture below.

John 16:33

These things I have spoken unto you, that in me ye might have peace. In the world ye shall have tribulation: but be of good cheer; I have overcome the world.

Using the MPS System™, you'd simply break this scripture down. (See example below).

	Meditation Points
1	These things I have spoken.
2	These things I have spoken unto you.
3	In me, you might have peace.
4	In the world, you will have tribulation.
5	But, be of good cheer.
6	Be of good cheer.
7	I have overcome.
8	I have overcome the world.

As you can see, I was able to extract eight pointers or points from John 16:33. Next, you'd find one or more keywords that stand out. This will help you to remember and extract the revelation from the scriptures you're meditating on. For example, the keyword that I'd focus on in the aforementioned scripture would be "overcome," so I'd look for scriptures that mention the word "overcome" (in present or past tense). A quick search engine search helped me to come up with the following:

Romans 12:21	Do not be overcome by evil, but overcome evil with good.
1 John 5:4	For everyone born of God overcomes the world. This is the victory that has overcome the world, even our faith.
Romans 8:37	No, in all these things we are more than conquerors through him who loved us.
1 John 4:4	You, dear children, are from God and have overcome them, because the one who is in you is greater than the one who is in the world.
1 John 5:5	Who is it that overcomes the world? Only the one who believes that Jesus is the Son of God.

Note: the scriptures that I use don't necessarily have to have the exact keyword that I'm looking for. I can find scriptures that have words that are synonymous, for example, with the word "overcome."

I'd then take these scriptures and break them down into points. For example, let's break Romans 12:21 down.

Meditation Points
Do not be overcome.
Do not be overcome by evil.
Overcome evil.
Overcome evil with good.

You can spread this keyword over the span of a day, a week or a month. Lastly, conduct a search for the keyword. For example, I could look up the etymology of the word "overcome" and this is what I'd find.

Overcome (Etymology)
Old English ofercuman "to reach, overtake, move or pass over," also "to conquer, prevail over, defeat in combat" (the Devil, evil spirits, sin, temptation, etc.), from ofer (see over) + cuman "to come" (see come (v.)). A common Germanic compound (Middle Dutch overkomen, Old High German ubarqueman, German überkommen).

In reference to mental or chemical force, "to overwhelm, render helpless," it is in late Old English. Meaning "to surmount (a difficulty or obstacle); succeed, be successful" is from c. 1200. The Civil Rights anthem "We Shall Overcome" was put together c. 1950s from the lyrics of Charles Tindley's spiritual "I'll Overcome Some Day" (1901) and the melody from the pre-Civil War spiritual "No More Auction Block for Me." Related: Overcame; overcoming.

Source: Online Etymology Dictionary

Note: the goal isn't just to hear or read a word, but it's to get understanding. One of the greatest hindrances to growth is a lack of understanding. We often read words that we don't fully understand. We have a surface-level grasp of what certain words mean, but we don't necessarily understand the depth of each word. A simple search from your favorite search engine could give you a lot of insight into what you're reading in your Bible. If you want to go deeper, look up the Greek and Hebrew definition for each keyword. You can continue extracting keywords and breaking them down until you're ready to move on to another subject or scripture.

Breathing Techniques

There are many breathing techniques that you can utilize while meditating and reflecting. Below, you'll find four really effective breathing techniques that you can incorporate into your studies.

Pursed Lip Breathing

This is a simple breathing technique that makes you focus on every individual breath. By doing this, you will intentionally slow down your breathing pace.

Steps

1. Relax.
2. Keeping your mouth closed, inhale two times slowly through your nose.
3. Purse or pucker your lips like you're about to whistle.
4. Exhale slowly through your mouth for a count of four.

Diaphragmatic Breathing

Diaphragmatic breathing (also known as belly breathing) requires you to fully engage your stomach, your abdominal muscles and your diaphragm. The goal is to fill your lungs with air and to fully engage your diaphragm while breathing.

Steps

1. Place one or two pillows beneath your knees.

2. Place a pillow under your head and lie down on a flat surface.
3. Place one hand on the middle of your chest.
4. Place your other hand on your stomach (an inch beneath the rib cage, but just above your diaphragm).
5. Breathe in through your nose, pulling your breath down towards your stomach.
6. Exhale by tightening your abdominal muscles and allowing your stomach to shrink. Allow your breath to escape through your pursed lips.

Deep Breathing

Deep breathing is popular for people who have trouble breathing. All the same, it increases the amount of oxygen that flows to the brain.

Steps

1. This exercise can be done while standing or sitting. Allow your chest to expand by pulling your elbows back.
2. Inhale through your nose.
3. Hold your breath for a total of five seconds.
4. Exhale through your nose.

Breath Focus Technique

This popular technique requires you to use your imagination! Your goal is to focus on words, phrases or images. For example, think of a scripture or a story in the Bible. Focus on that thought for ten or more minutes. You can increase this time as you go along.

Steps

1. Sit or lie down.
2. Concentrate on your breaths.
3. Alternate between normal and deep breaths.
4. Let out an audible sigh every time you exhale.
5. Combine these steps with images or scriptures.

Please note that it is not mandatory or necessary for you to involve any of these techniques in your meditation or reflection time. The main goal is to be comfortable. This would allow you to relax more, which of course would equate to a better breathing experience.

THE REVELATION OF BREATH

We take in air through our respiratory system. This system is made up of three dimensions or parts; they are: the airway, the lungs and the muscles used for breathing. The airway is comprised of your nose, mouth, throat and trachea (windpipe). Your lungs pull air into your body, and from there, it enters your trachea. Your nose doesn't have a filtering system, so any air that passes into your body has to be filtered by your blood. Please note that when we inhale, we breathe in air that is approximately 20.95% oxygen, 78.09% nitrogen, 0.93% argon, and 0.04% carbon dioxide. Once the air enters the blood, it is then filtered. Carbon dioxide is a waste product, so it is sent back through the trachea, where it reenters the lungs and is then exhaled. The muscles in our respiratory system help to control our breathing. The main muscle is what we call our diaphragm. Of course, there are other muscles that assist the diaphragm, including muscles in our chest and stomach.

We need air to live; this is just how we were designed. As a matter of fact, there are two types of legal terms that doctors use to officiate a legal death. They are:

1. **Cardiopulmonary Death:** The individual's heartbeat and breathing have ceased, and this cessation is determined to be irreversible.
2. **Brain Death:** The functions of the individual's brain have ceased, and this inactivity is determined to be irreversible.

In truth, death is simply the inability to breathe. Remember, God breathed the breath of life into Adam's lungs, but before He did this, Adam was lifeless. So, when mankind sinned against God, God simply withdrew Himself from mankind. Simply put, man is a spirit. He is a breath of God, so he can never cease to exist. (The same is true of angels.) When God removed Himself from mankind, He didn't remove man's ability to breathe (live). Instead, He removed His nature (holiness) from mankind, since man had sinned against Him and would then bear the nature of sin. Adam's job at that point was to study the mind and movements of God, and to replicate or express what he saw God do in the Earth's realm. This was the birth of religion. Religion is performance-based. All the same, religion did not justify the man, it simply condemned him since mankind was shaped in iniquity. Sin would ultimately bring about the first death, but remember, this didn't mean that the spirit of the man ceased to exist. He simply stopped living in the earth suit (flesh) that had been loaned to him. Your earth suit is what legalizes your existence in the Earth's realm. Once man leaves his earth suit behind, his spirit then returns to God; this is the process of God inhaling, and if that man's name is not found in the Lamb's Book of Life, God then exhales. In other words, the spirit of the man is expressed as waste and must go into utter (complete) darkness where the Bible says there is weeping and gnashing of teeth. Howbeit, darkness is not what we think it is. God is Light; we've already come to this determination. And remember, darkness was not created by God. It does not exist, meaning, it is lifeless, however, it can be seen. Darkness is unoccupied space; it is space that has not been filled with God's presence. Think of it this way—if you ordered a book from Amazon and they shipped it to you in a large box, what you'll see when you open the box is a lot of space. You'll notice that they'll attempt to fill that space with air pillows and/or foam, both of which are cheap materials. But the box probably won't be completely filled, so when the box is closed, it will be mostly filled with darkness. If you were to x-ray the box, you'd see quite a bit of darkness. This is because you can't place God in a box (think religion).

The Genesis of a Breath

In the beginning God created the heaven and the earth.

Genesis (Etymology)

Old English Genesis, first book of the Pentateuch, which tells among other things of the creation of the world, from Latin genesis "generation, nativity," in Late Latin taken as the title of first book of the Old Testament, from Greek genesis "origin, creation, generation," from gignesthai "to be born," related to genos "race, birth, descent" (from PIE root *gene- "give birth, beget," with derivatives referring to procreation and familial and tribal groups). Greek translators used the word as the title of the biblical book, rendering Hebrew bereshith, literally "in the beginning," which was the first word of the text, taken as its title. Extended sense of "origin, creation" first recorded in English c. 1600.

Source: Online Etymology Dictionary

The Greek word for "génesis" simply means "origin." It's where we get the words gene, generation and genetics. "In the beginning, God created the heaven and the earth." Who is YAHWEH? He answers this question for us in Revelation 22:13. He said,

"I am Alpha and Omega, the beginning and the end, the first and the last."

So, when the scripture says, "In the beginning, God created the Heaven and the Earth," it wasn't denoting Chronos time, since time had not yet been created. This scripture represents a locale.

- God is the Beginning.
- He created the Heavens and the Earth inside of Himself.

Who is God? He is the multidimensional, multifaceted Source (Abba) of everything. Romans 8:15 reads, "The Spirit you received does not make you slaves, so that you live in fear again; rather, the Spirit you received brought about your adoption to sonship. And by him we cry, "Abba, Father."

Abba (Etymology)
Biblical title of honor, literally "father," used as an invocation of God, from Latin abba, from Greek abba, from Aramaic (Semitic) abba "the father, my father," emphatic state of abh "father." Also a title in the Syriac and Coptic churches.
It is used in the New Testament three times (Mark xiv. 36, Rom. viii. 15, Gal. iv. 6), in each instance accompanied by its translation, "Abba, Father," as an invocation of the Deity, expressing close filial relation. Either through its liturgical use in the Judeo-Christian church or through its employment by the Syriac monks, it has passed into general ecclesiastical language in the modified form of abbat or abbot .... [Century Dictionary]
Source: Online Etymology Dictionary

Front of God	Back of God
Alpha	Omega
Beginning	End
Genesis	Revelation
Abba (Father)	Jesus (Son)

In the beginning, God created the Heavens and the Earth. In the beginning, God created man. Everything God created, He created within Himself (idea), and then He pulled it out of Himself (creation), but He didn't use His hands, after all, He is Spirit. John 4:24 says, "God is a Spirit: and they that worship him must worship him in spirit and in truth," but other translations, including the New King James version of the Bible says it this way, "God is Spirit," removing the word "a" because it unintentionally implies that every other spirit is on the same spectrum or level as Him, and we all know that this is not true. Satan is not on the same level as God, and while he is the "prince of this world," God is the King of kings and Lord of lords. In other words, God and Satan are not equal in height, dimension, rank or abilities. Satan is a creature, meaning he was created just like the rest of us. YAHWEH, on the other hand, is the Source (Abba/Father) of all things. So, He is Spirit, and every other extension of His breath is "a spirit," including Lucifer himself. Let's look at the word "spirit" to get more insight into its meaning.

Spirit (Etymology)
mid-13c., "animating or vital principle in man and animals," from Anglo-French spirit, Old French espirit "spirit, soul" (12c., Modern French esprit) and directly from Latin spiritus "a breathing (respiration, and of the wind), breath; breath of a god," hence "inspiration; breath of

Spirit (Etymology)
life," hence "life;" also "disposition, character; high spirit, vigor, courage; pride, arrogance," related to spirare "to breathe," perhaps from PIE *(s)peis- "to blow" (source also of Old Church Slavonic pisto "to play on the flute"). But de Vaan says "Possibly an onomatopoeic formation imitating the sound of breathing. There are no direct cognates." Meaning "supernatural immaterial creature; angel, demon; an apparition, invisible corporeal being of an airy nature" is attested from mid-14c.; from late 14c. as "a ghost" (see ghost (n.)). From c. 1500 as "a nature, character"; sense of "essential principle of something" (in a non-theological context, as in Spirit of St. Louis) is attested from 1680s, common after 1800; Spirit of '76 in reference to the qualities that sparked and sustained the American Revolution is attested by 1797 in William Cobbett's "Porcupine's Gazette and Daily Advertiser."
Source: Online Etymology Dictionary

Spirit	
Hebrew	**Greek**
Ruach	Pneuma
Definition: breath, wind, spirit	

Knowing now what we've read about the word "spirit" and who God is, let's take another look at Genesis 1:1-2. "In the beginning God created the Heavens and the Earth. And the Earth was without form, and void; and darkness [was] upon the face of the deep. And the Spirit of God moved upon the face of the waters." The Spirit or, better yet, breath, wind or expression of God moved upon the face of the waters which, of course, were covered by darkness. John 1:1-5 says, "In the beginning was the Word, and the Word was with God, and the Word was God. The same was in the beginning with God. All things were made by him; and without him was not anything made that was made. In Him was life; and the life was the light of men. And the light shineth in darkness; and the darkness comprehended it not." So, in Genesis 1, we witness God moving upon the face of darkness, but according to John 1, the darkness did not recognize Him. If darkness existed outside of God and it did not recognize Him, how did darkness come to be? It's simple. God is Light; the scriptures tell us this, but how can He call Himself Light or even acknowledge and express His identity if there was nothing for Him to distinguish Himself from? Simply put, the word "dark" simply means "void" or "absent of light/life." It means that something hasn't yet been touched by God or God has withdrew Himself from a thing. Darkness doesn't have a personality, a will or a voice. It represents an empty space, a capacity and even an opportunity for God to express Himself. John 1 says, "Without Him was not anything made that was made." One (modern day) rule of writing is to never use two negative terms in a sentence because it confuses western readers. So, a more understood way of saying this would be:

- "Everything that was made or created was created inside of Him."
- "Nothing (darkness) was made outside of Him."
- "Anything created outside of Him is dark (illegal)."

The word "without" means "outside of." Remember, He created the Heavens and the Earth "in the beginning" or, better yet, inside of Himself. Howbeit, outside of Himself or without His expression, life, permission, there was no existence. He is the Creator, Source and Father of all things. So, when He stood over Adam and began to form him, He was performing the same actions He'd performed over the face of the deep. Man was without form and void, and darkness or, better yet, lifelessness was upon the face of the deep (dust). So, God "formed" man out of the dust of the ground, but man was still lifeless (void) and without expression (life). God then made an impartation. Genesis 2:7 tells us what took place that memorable day in the Garden. "And the LORD God formed man of the dust of the ground and breathed into his nostrils the breath of life; and man became a living soul." When God breathed into man, He was pretty much saying, "Let there be light" or "Let there be life." Adam then became a "living soul," meaning he became animated and began to express himself through movements. In layman's terms, Adam became an extension of God's breath or Spirit!

The Greek word for "soul" is "psuche," and it literally means "breath." God then put His breath (Adam) to work. He blew on the Garden of Eden or, better yet, He placed Adam in the Garden to dress it. Attached to his ability to express himself, Adam also had another ability called "will." It was the same ability God had given His angels and, of course, Lucifer had abused that privilege by operating outside of God's will. In other words, Lucifer (the light bringer or light bearer) decided to operate in darkness. This means that Lucifer did not create darkness, he simply went outside the will of God to express himself, and it was in the darkness that he misrepresented God. Nevertheless, there Adam stood in the Garden of Eden, and God then gave him his first assignment. He was completely oblivious to the kingdom of darkness. All he knew was that God told him that he could eat from every tree in the Garden except for the Tree of the Knowledge of Good and Evil. He had no reason to doubt God; he had no reason to question God. Instead, he went to work. Genesis 2:18-20 reads, "And the LORD God said, It is not good that the man should be alone; I will make him an help meet for him. And out of the ground the LORD God formed every beast of the field, and every fowl of the air; and brought them unto Adam to see what he would call them: and whatsoever Adam called every living creature, that was the name thereof. And Adam gave names to all cattle, and to the fowl of the air, and to every beast of the field; but for Adam there was not found a help meet for him." In this, we witness God identifying another void, and that was the absence of woman. God is good; we all know this, but He said, "It is not good for man to be alone." In other words, it is outside of His will for man to be alone. This doesn't mean that every man or woman needs to be married; it simply means that every man and woman needs a community. But before He answered Adam's void, He gave him an assignment. He brought the animals that He'd created to Adam to see what he would call them. In short, God was trying to see if Adam was connected to Him enough or mature enough to handle his next role. Adam passed the test; he called the animals what God had already called them, and this is when Adam became a source (small letters). God put Adam to sleep and pulled Eve out of him. Eve then became a resource, meaning, she had to draw from the source to express herself (reproduce). Before long, there were two expressions of God breathing in the Garden. One was directly connected to the Source, while the other was connected to a source.

The Breath of Life	
Genesis 2:7	And the Lord God formed man of the dust of the ground, and breathed into his nostrils the breath of life; and man became a living soul.
Genesis 6:17	And, behold, I, even I, do bring a flood of waters upon the earth, to destroy all flesh, wherein is the breath of life, from under heaven; and every thing that is in the earth shall die.
Genesis 7:15	And they went in unto Noah into the ark, two and two of all flesh, wherein is the breath of life.
Job 33:4	The spirit of God hath made me, and the breath of the Almighty hath given me life
John 1:4	In him was life; and the life was the light of men.

There are a lot of terms that are now being used by New Agers, with one of those terms being the word "energy." Because of this, most of the church has distanced themselves from this term, along with other words like vibrations, consciousness and holistic. Please understand that these are mere words; they are a part of our (not so largely used) vocabulary. And not only that, they've been around for thousands of years. But what the New Age movement is doing is taking Christian concepts and labeling them by using words that we use infrequently. In essence, the enemy is gaining ground while the church seems to be losing ground. Think of the box concept. Inside of a large box, you may find the book that you ordered, but if there's nothing else in that box, the packagers will fill it with useless materials like air pillows and/or foam. All of the darkness (space, opportunities) that we, as the church, refuse to fill (occupy, claim), Satan will lord himself over and fill it with useless, powerless doctrines of devils and darkness. Let's deal with and take back the word "energy" to start with.

Energy (Etymology)
1590s, "force of expression," from Middle French énergie (16c.), from Late Latin energia, from Greek energeia "activity, action, operation," from energos "active, working," from en "at" (see en- (2)) + ergon "work, that which is wrought; business; action," from PIE root *werg- "to do." Used by Aristotle with a sense of "actuality, reality, existence" (opposed to "potential") but this was misunderstood in Late Latin and afterward as "force of expression," as the power which calls up realistic mental pictures. Broader meaning of "power" in English is first recorded 1660s. Scientific use is from 1807. Energy crisis first attested 1970.
Source: Online Etymology Dictionary

There are two main types of energy that have been identified by scientists. They are:
1. **Potential Energy:** This is stored energy that has not yet been used.
2. **Kinetic Energy:** Energy that has been used or is currently in use.

Energy, by scientific standards, is the ability to do work. It's the ability to move a thing or to influence movement. Think about the domino effect. If you take a few dominoes, stand them up and place them within reach of one another, they all have the ability to affect or impact one another. This is called potential energy. But because they are lifeless, they will continue standing unless they are on an imbalanced plane or unless they are moved by force (kinetic energy). Because they are nearly weightless, it doesn't take much energy to knock them over. So, if you (slightly) push one of the dominoes in the direction of the other dominoes, the force of gravity will take effect and the energy from your finger will be transferred to the domino, causing it to fall. When it hits the neighboring domino, that energy will be transferred to that particular one, thus, causing it to fall. As the dominoes fall, they create friction, causing some of the energy to be converted into heat and sound. This will continue until all of the dominoes are resting (lifeless) on whatever surface you've placed them on. Once the last domino falls, the energy doesn't evaporate or cease to exist, the dominoes continue to house potential. Meaning, you can stand them up again and replicate the same experiment.

Think about food. Whatever you eat will be broken down by your respiratory system; some of it may be converted into energy, some of it may be stored as fat and the rest will be converted into waste. This waste will be expelled from your body in a process that we call a bowel movement.

Energy has five uses in the human body. They are:

1. **Basic or Basal Metabolism:** This is the minimum amount of energy that your body needs to survive, especially when the body is at rest.

2. **Digestion and Nutrient Absorption:** Digestion is the chemical breakdown of the foods that we've ingested, but absorption is a process by which nutrients, water and electrolytes move from the small intestine and into the blood, where it is then converted into energy.

3. **Physical Energy:** We work, we move around, and we play, and whatever energy we don't work off, we have to (or should be) burning through exercise, otherwise, it will be stored as fat. Fat is similar to the foam found in boxes that is used to fill the unoccupied spaces.

4. **Mental Energy:** Believe it or not, our minds need energy too. As a matter of fact, our brains require a tremendous amount of energy to function. This is because everything we do with our minds require energy, including working, doing homework, exercising, reading, learning, communicating and the list is endless.

5. **Body Composition:** Your body composition is the proportion of fat versus non-fat mass in your body. Your body composition is a major factor in determining how much energy your body needs. For example, men are typically more muscular than women, and therefore, require more calories than women. Consequently, you'll find that men tend to eat more than women. A healthy body composition is one that consists of a lower percentage of body fat and a higher percentage of fat-free mass (bones, organs, muscle).

Another word for "energy" is "power." When God breathed the breath of life into Adam, he became a living (energetic, animated) soul. The energy that moved through his body is what we call life. Adam became a "living" soul. In other words, he became energized. His limbs started moving, his neurons started firing and everything in him started functioning. Before God breathed into Adam's lungs, Adam was just a form of godliness, but he had no power (energy) to deny. Once Adam died, his spirit didn't cease to exist. It simply left his body and returned to God to be judged. The First Law of Thermodynamics (coined in 1842 by Julius Robert Mayer) states this fact— "Energy is neither created nor destroyed." This is true in the Earth's realm, but not so true when dealing with the spirit realm. When Adam sinned, he created the domino effect. Every child born to him would bear his iniquities. This chain reaction would continue until the death and resurrection of Jesus Christ. And while we are still impacted by sin, as believers, our spirits (energies) are no longer subject to the kingdom of darkness. So, when we take our last breath in the Earth, God inhales us; in other words, we return to Him, and He expresses us in His Kingdom. Colossians 1:12-13 says it this way, "Giving thanks unto the Father, which hath made us meet to be partakers of the inheritance of the <u>saints in light</u>:

Who hath delivered us <u>from the power of darkness</u>, and hath <u>translated</u> us into the kingdom of his dear Son" Simply put, while the domino (human) still falls in the Earth's realm, it falls in a different direction (because of repentance) so that it can stand in the Kingdom of God.

Before we go any further, let's establish this fact—God is not an enemy of science and science is not an enemy of God. True science proves the existence of God, but whenever science appears to disprove His existence, the science is not true, but is being manipulated, misunderstood or misrepresented by the scientist. Scientists are encouraged to be unbiased, but we all know that many of them are biased. Many of them have already settled on the belief that God doesn't exist; this is largely due to them wanting to be accepted in the ranks of the scientific community, so when their research starts pointing to the existence of God, they intentionally and maliciously attempt to manipulate the research. Think of it this way—if a new scientist admires, envies or even idolizes a well-known scientific voice, and that scientist's lifelong dream is to teach alongside his idol, do you truly believe that the rookie will publish evidence that contradicts the work or theories of the expert? Some would, but many would not. When true scientists retest and disprove theories and laws established by their predecessors, they are taking huge risks career-wise. Many of the bolder ones establish new theories, some of which could eventually become scientific laws. This can and does create a rift in the scientific community, with most scientists siding with the expert, even though the evidence supports the claims of the non-expert. Most rookies are not willing to challenge a well-known theory or voice because of this.

Again, according to science, energy is neither created, nor is it destroyed. While this can be proven in the realm of the Earth, it is not entirely true when dealing with the topic of spirituality. Energy was created by God, and bad energy (spirits) will be destroyed in Hades. But the concept of destruction is not mere death (the loss of consciousness); instead, it means to be separated from or divorced by God—forever! It means to be outside of the presence of God—forever! It means to be cast into utter darkness (a space not used or filled by God)—forever! It means to be a created thing without its Creator—forever! All the same, it means to be conscious of your separation from God and all that He is (good, faithful, holy)—forever! Your spirit is energy; it is your life-force. It cannot cease to exist, so it has to be housed in eternity. Now that we understand this, let's come to understand the concept of spirituality. In layman's terms, spirituality is the belief in a higher power. As Christians, we believe in YAHWEH. He is not just a "higher power," He is the King of kings, the Lord of lords, the Creator of all things, including Heaven and Earth. Many alternate faiths believe in other powers or deities, and while many of these "lords" do exist (anything you worship, by default, becomes at minimum, your god), they are all lower than God because He created them. Hear me—God created Lucifer! When He created Lucifer, which means "light-bearer," Lucifer wasn't evil! The same is true for the angels that fell with him. They were all "light-bearers." However, they desired to be gods; they wanted to be esteemed, worshiped and feared. Consequently, God removed His light (presence) from them, and this is how they became dark. Needless to say, they can be rendered as gods, even though they were created by God. The evidence can be found in Romans 1.

Romans 1:18-32

For the wrath of God is revealed from heaven against all ungodliness and unrighteousness of men, who hold the truth in unrighteousness; because that which may be known of God is manifest in them; for God hath shewed it unto them. For the invisible things of him from the creation of the world are clearly seen, being understood by the things that are made, even his eternal power and Godhead; so that they are without excuse: Because that, when they knew God, they glorified him not as God, neither were thankful; but became vain in their imaginations, and their foolish heart was darkened. Professing themselves to be wise, they became fools, and changed the glory of the uncorruptible God into an image made like to corruptible man, and to birds, and four-footed beasts, and creeping things.

Wherefore God also gave them up to uncleanness through the lusts of their own hearts, to dishonor their own bodies between themselves: Who changed the truth of God into a lie, and worshiped and served the creature more than the Creator, who is blessed forever. Amen. For this cause God gave them up unto vile affections: for even their women did change the natural use into that which is against nature: And likewise also the men, leaving the natural use of the woman, burned in their lust one toward another; men with men working that which is unseemly, and receiving in themselves that recompense of their error which was meet. And even as they did not like to retain God in their knowledge, God gave them over to a reprobate mind, to do those things which are not convenient; being filled with all unrighteousness, fornication, wickedness, covetousness, maliciousness; full of envy, murder, debate, deceit, malignity; whisperers, backbiters, haters of God, despiteful, proud, boasters, inventors of evil things, disobedient to parents, without understanding, covenant-breakers, without natural affection, implacable, unmerciful: Who knowing the judgment of God, that they which commit such things are worthy of death, not only do the same, but have pleasure in them that do them.

Hear me—Lucifer was and is a spirit! He is a breath, but he became bad (evil) when he looked into the secrets of God and saw something that he was supposed to cover! Before we delve deeper into this mystery, let's establish this fact—spirits are energies; they are the breaths of God, and like He did with mankind, He gave spirits the engine of will. This means that they can make a decision independent of God's influence, even though doing so would cost them greatly. God is like many of us or, better yet, most of us are like God—we don't want anyone who doesn't want us! This is why the whole concept of romantic witchcraft is foolish. Why would you bewitch someone into wanting you?! God wants us to want Him back! He wants us to want Him soberly, but in order for us to do this, we have to get to know Him intimately. Otherwise, we'll romanticize the concept of God and Heaven, and thus, enter into religiousness. Being religious means attempting to fill with empty space (void) with works, rather than having the substance of things hoped for and the evidence of things not seen which, of course, is faith! But an intimate knowledge of God gives way to an intimate relationship with God; this is what causes us to "know Him" and soberly choose Him as Lord over our lives. This is what it means to have faith. In other words, religion cannot replace relationship.

What then is the breath of life? If the word "breath" means "spirit" and God is "life," could it be that the breath of life is the Spirit of God? And when God removed His Spirit from mankind, He simply separated His Spirit from our spirit. When Jesus died and was resurrected for us, He simply reconciled our spirit with God's Spirit. This means that we no longer have to subject ourselves to works (the religious expression of energy), but we would be influenced, led and saved by the power of God. We became like oxygen, but unbelievers became like carbon dioxide. God inhaled us into His body to express us in His Kingdom, whereas, the workers of iniquity are exhaled into the kingdom of darkness.

Good Breath

YAHWEH breathed the breath of life into the nostrils of Adam. And because He is good, it goes without saying that the breath He breathed into Adam was and is good. Anytime God breathes on something, He is imparting in and of Himself; He is releasing good. Adam was a good breath until he contaminated himself with lies. Let me explain.

First, hold your breath and try to speak. What you'll notice is that this is nearly impossible, and it's something you can't do for too long. All the same, you'll notice that a little air escapes your lungs to aid you in carrying out the task. Without your breath, your tongue has the ability to move, but it cannot produce sound on its own. This is because your lungs must produce a sufficient amount of airflow and air pressure in order for them to cause your vocal cords to vibrate. With this said, sound and air are connected. Now, let's look at what took place in the Garden between Satan and Eve. Genesis 3:1 reads, "Now the serpent was more subtil than any beast of the field which the LORD God had made. And he said unto the woman, Yea, hath God said, Ye shall not eat of every tree of the garden?" What's happening here? First, you'll notice that Satan is using the body of a serpent. This is because he is powerless. He needs a body (energy source) to operate in the realm of the Earth. Next, the Bible tells us about the snake; it deals with the beast or animal itself, calling it more subtil than any beast of the field. The word "subtil" means cunning. This means that it was more intelligent than most animals. And like the other animals, snakes had the ability to choose (will). But that snake chose to allow itself to be used by Satan (consequently, it lost its legs and was cast onto its belly). Satan borrowed the snake's body so that he could talk with Eve. Remember, God had given mankind dominion over the beasts of the field. In other words, Eve stood there and took spiritual advice from something that had lower rank than herself. When Satan opened his mouth, he released a bad breath because he was and is an evil spirit. How do we respond when someone with bad breath starts talking with us? We cover our noses because we don't want to inhale the smell. We also put distance between ourselves and the person, and in some cases, we may even offer the person gum or make the individual aware of the halitosis. But Eve didn't do this. Let's look at how she responded. Genesis 3:2-7 reads, "And the woman said unto the serpent, We may eat of the fruit of the trees of the garden: But of the fruit of the tree which is in the midst of the garden, God hath said, Ye shall not eat of it, neither shall ye touch it, lest ye die. And the serpent said unto the woman, Ye shall not surely die: For God doth know that in the day ye eat thereof, then your eyes shall be opened, and ye shall be as gods, knowing good and evil. And when the woman saw that the tree was good for food, and that it was pleasant to the eyes, and a tree to be desired to make one wise, she took of the fruit thereof, and did eat, and gave also unto her husband with her; and he did eat. And the eyes of them both were opened, and they knew that they were naked; and they sewed fig leaves together, and made themselves aprons."

First and foremost, we've all been taught to not talk with strangers. Eve knew what God said; she had her set of instructions, so when a contrary wind began to blow in her ears, she should have responded the way Jesus responded when Satan tempted Him in the wilderness. She should have said:

- "Man shall not live by bread alone, but by every word that proceedeth out of the mouth of God."
- "Thou shalt not tempt the Lord thy God."
- "Get thee hence, Satan: for it is written, Thou shalt worship the Lord thy God, and him only shalt thou serve."

Nevertheless, she stood there and inhaled the bad breath. She took in the lies and exhaled the truth. After this happened, she seduced her husband into disobeying God, and man fell as a result of their rebellion. God removed His Spirit from man, but man didn't cease to be a spirit. Mankind simply became unholy. A little more than thousand years later, God fulfilled His Word that He would send mankind a Redeemer. Matthew 1:18 (ESV) reads, "Now the birth of Jesus

Christ took place in this way. When his mother Mary had been betrothed to Joseph, before they came together, she was found to be with child from the Holy Spirit." Remember, the Holy Spirit is the expression of God in the Earth. He is the Breath of Life, the eternal presence and power of God! Jesus increased in wisdom and stature, and in favor with God and man, and at the age of 30, Jesus was baptized. Luke 3:21-22 reads, "Now when all the people were baptized, it came to pass, that Jesus also being baptized, and praying, the heaven was opened, and the Holy Ghost descended in a bodily shape like a dove upon him, and a voice came from heaven, which said, Thou art my beloved Son; in thee I am well pleased." What happened here? The breath, life and everlasting power of God came upon Jesus! Jesus was and is the expressed power of God in the Earth; He is a good breath! But man was dark; mankind was condemned because of sin, and in order for us to be saved, we desperately needed the Holy Spirit. And in order for us to receive the Holy Spirit, Jesus would have to fulfill His assignment. He would have to die and be resurrected. John 7:37-39 reads, "In the last day, that great day of the feast, Jesus stood and cried, saying, If any man thirst, let him come unto me, and drink. He that believeth on me, as the scripture hath said, out of his belly shall flow rivers of living water. (But this spake he of the Spirit, which they that believe on him should receive: for the Holy Ghost was not yet given; because that Jesus was not yet glorified.)"

Eventually, Jesus was glorified and when He returned, He breathed upon or imparted the Holy Spirit into some of His disciples. Let's look at a few scriptures.

John 20:19-23

Then the same day at evening, being the first day of the week, when the doors were shut where the disciples were assembled for fear of the Jews, came Jesus and stood in the midst, and saith unto them, Peace be unto you. And when he had so said, he shewed unto them his hands and his side. Then were the disciples glad, when they saw the Lord. Then said Jesus to them again, Peace be unto you: as my Father hath sent me, even so send I you. And when he had said this, he breathed on them, and saith unto them, Receive ye the Holy Ghost: Whose soever sins ye remit, they are remitted unto them; and whose soever sins ye retain, they are retained.

Acts 2:1-4

And when the day of Pentecost was fully come, they were all with one accord in one place. And suddenly there came a sound from heaven as of a rushing mighty wind, and it filled all the house where they were sitting. And there appeared unto them cloven tongues like as of fire, and it sat upon each of them. And they were all filled with the Holy Ghost, and began to speak with other tongues, as the Spirit gave them utterance.

In this, we see that the Good Breath or Holy Spirit of God was reconciled with those who accepted Jesus Christ as their Lord and Savior. Howbeit, the reconciliation of man with God did not put an end to the kingdom of darkness; instead, God separated (sanctified) us from it.

Bad Breath

We've all had it—halitosis or bad breath. There are many ways that bad breath can form. The chart below lists the origins of bad breath.

Origins	Revelation
Food	Whatever you consume will eventually express itself through your mouth. Think of food. Some of what you eat will be converted to energy, some of what you eat will be converted to fat (unspent energy) and the rest will be converted to waste. The same is true for words. Whatever you allow into your heart will eventually express itself through your mouth and your choices. Your mouth can be seen as the digestive tract (rectum) of your heart.
Poor Dental Hygiene	This represents self-control. Your teeth are the gates around your tongue. Whatever you allow past them will get into your belly (the heart of your flesh) and eventually begin to express itself through your limbs (members). Additionally, processed foods and poor hygiene would eventually corrode the enamel around your teeth, causing tooth loss and decay. This means that you wouldn't be able to eat certain foods anymore. Think of this on a spiritual plane. God told us to guard our hearts, for out of it, He says, are the issues of life. When a person fails to guard his or her heart, that person, in turn, subjects himself or herself to an uncontrolled diet of good and bad, darkness and light. In other words, the person lacks self-control. This would corrode the person's ability to discern good from evil through a process called desensitization (numbness). Consequently, the individual would become double-minded and unstable in all his or her ways. The more teeth or, better yet, self-control the person loses, the more likely the individual is to defile himself/herself. Matthew 15:10-11 says, "And he called the people to him and said to them, 'Hear and understand: it is not what goes into the mouth that defiles a person, but what comes out of the mouth; this defiles a person.'" In this, the Lord was dealing with the breath or expression of a man's heart, since whatever it is that he speaks, he has given weight to. In

Origins	Revelation
	other words, he allows it to go past his gates (teeth) so that it can reproduce itself.
Medications	Another word for "medication" or "drugs" is the Greek word "pharmakeia," which literally means "witchcraft." Witchcraft is another source or, better yet, an expression of power outside of God's influence or will. In the natural, medication is an external resource used to remedy or address an internal issue. When we use the word "pharmakeia" or "witchcraft," the author is dealing with a power not created "in the beginning," meaning it wasn't created inside the will of God or for the purpose of glorifying God; instead, it was created as an alternate means or source of power. It is an external expression used to address an internal issue. In other words, it is a foreign or bad breath.
Dry Mouth	This could represent keeping your mouth closed when it should be open. It means not having a word to speak in due season. Other words for this include passivity, impotence and fear.
Tobacco	Tobacco is a drug, so this could easily fall under "pharmakeia," but the difference is that this is a recreational drug, meaning, it's not used to address a problem. Instead, it's used for entertainment. Think about the entertainment industry. We go to church and read our Bibles to hear words of encouragement, edification and exhortation, but the mediums or, better yet, media often serves as a tool for the kingdom of darkness to express itself through. It's not a surprise that many believers are still being entertained and influenced by the expressions of darkness; this is largely because many Christians have yet to sanctify themselves from the world, therefore, they are still under the influence of the world's media (mediums).
Oral Infections	Oral infections are often caused by an internal source (overgrowth of certain types of bacteria) or an external source (foreign bacteria and viruses). Out of the abundance of the heart, the mouth speaks. Whatever you allow into your heart will behave much like a virus. It will attach itself to something healthy, corrupt it and then begin to reproduce itself. Consequently, when you open your mouth, whatever has filled your heart will begin to express itself. Undoubtedly, this is what happened to Lucifer. What he'd said in his heart (we'll deal with

Origins	Revelation
	this shortly) slowly but surely begin to express itself through his mouth.
Nasal, Sinus, Throat Inflammation	These are the instruments of breath. If any of them are corrupt, we will have bad breath or, better yet, a wrong or dark expression. All the same, when one of these is inflamed, the rest are impacted. This represents a system or cycle (habit, stronghold).
Other Diseases	It goes without saying that diseases are an invasion of otherwise healthy organs. So, in conclusion, this would be interpreted as demonic bondage.

All of the aforementioned issues are conduits of bad breath. If we look at the term "bad breath" spiritually, we could break it down this way:

- God is good.
- Anything outside of Him is bad.

Therefore, a bad breath is a spirit that expresses itself outside of YAHWEH's permission or influence. It is a contrary wind or contrary spirit, meaning, it is not for the Kingdom of God, therefore, it's against the Kingdom of God. Angels are spirits; they are the breaths of God working expressively inside and outside of the Earth's realm. There are good angels and there are bad angels (aka demons, devils, unclean spirits). In short, Satan is a breath gone bad. Demons (also known as devils) are also bad breaths. But how did they come to be, after all, they originated in God, right? Of course! Psalm 148:1-6 proves this; it reads, "Praise ye him, all his angels: praise ye him, all his hosts. Praise ye him, sun and moon: praise him, all ye stars of light. Praise him, ye heavens of heavens, and ye waters that be above the heavens. Let them praise the name of the LORD: for he commanded, and they were created. He hath also stablished them for ever and ever: he hath made a decree which shall not pass."

In the previous chapter, we determined that the word "spirit" means "breath" or "wind." We also determined that darkness is not a tangible expression of anything. It is the opposite of who God is; it means the absence of light, life, love or revelation. It means something that has no form, no power, no purpose and no movement. It is uncharted territory. Darkness doesn't "exist" per se; in simplistic terms, it's just open space outside of God. You can't bottle it up, lock it into a confined space or grasp it. It simply shows up when there is unoccupied space. Think about it this way. If someone gave you a house that was ten thousand square feet in measurement, and that house had fifteen bedrooms, would you be able to fill all of those rooms? Eventually, you may be able to, but as of right now, most of those rooms would remain empty. Each empty room represents potential. An empty space is subject to mold and squatters. This is because empty rooms are often left in the dark, and the moisture that collects in those rooms in the winter months can encourage the growth of mold and mildew. Additionally, squatters are known to move into empty rooms if the house is big enough for them to go undetected.

Remember, we've already established that spirits are breaths of God. Demons are spirits that chose to stray away from God. Consequently, He divorced them. This means that they are no longer good (they don't have His essence or His image). Instead, they are bad; another word for bad is evil. All the same, God is Light, so when He removed His presence from Satan and his cohorts, they lost the light that radiated through them. This is how they became dark. But what happened? How did they fall? What was their crime?

Isaiah 14:12-15

How art thou fallen from heaven, O Lucifer, son of the morning! How art thou cut down to the ground, which didst weaken the nations! For thou hast said in thine heart, I will ascend into heaven, I will exalt my throne above the stars of God: I will sit also upon the mount of the congregation, in the sides of the north: I will ascend above the heights of the clouds; I will be like the most High. Yet thou shalt be brought down to hell, to the sides of the pit.

Ezekiel 28:13-18

Thou hast been in Eden the garden of God; every precious stone was thy covering, the sardius, topaz, and the diamond, the beryl, the onyx, and the jasper, the sapphire, the emerald, and the carbuncle, and gold: the workmanship of thy tabrets and of thy pipes was prepared in thee in the day that thou wast created. Thou art the anointed cherub that covereth; and I have set thee so: thou wast upon the holy mountain of God; thou hast walked up and down in the midst of the stones of fire. Thou wast perfect in thy ways from the day that thou wast created, till iniquity was found in thee. By the multitude of thy merchandise they have filled the midst of thee with violence, and thou hast sinned: therefore I will cast thee as profane out of the mountain of God: and I will destroy thee, O covering cherub, from the midst of the stones of fire. Thine heart was lifted up because of thy beauty, thou hast corrupted thy wisdom by reason of thy brightness: I will cast thee to the ground, I will lay thee before kings, that they may behold thee. Thou hast defiled thy sanctuaries by the multitude of thine iniquities, by the iniquity of thy traffick; therefore will I bring forth a fire from the midst of thee, it shall devour thee, and I will bring thee to ashes upon the earth in the sight of all them that behold thee.

Notice that the aforementioned scripture referred to him as the covering cherub, but what was he covering? Before we go any further into this, let's look at the word "merchandise" since the scripture says, "By the multitude of thy merchandise they have filled the midst of thee with violence." What does this mean? The word "merchandise" comes from the Hebrew word "rekullah" and it literally means "traffic." This is where we get the words "traffic" and "trafficking." Another word for "trafficking" is "trade," but what was Lucifer trading or selling? Romans 1:21-25 (ESV) gives us some insight. It reads, "For although they knew God, they did not honor him as God or give thanks to him, but they became futile in their thinking, and their foolish hearts were darkened. Claiming to be wise, they became fools, and exchanged the glory of the immortal God for images resembling mortal man and birds and animals and creeping things. Therefore God gave them up in the lusts of their hearts to impurity, to the dishonoring of their bodies among themselves, because they exchanged the truth about God for a lie and worshiped and served the creature rather than the Creator, who is blessed forever! Amen." And while this scripture deals with unrighteous men and women, please note that God said they'd made an exchange. Who did they make this exchange with? Satan, of course! But this wasn't the first time Satan had done this! He'd perverted one third of God's angels, causing them to fall away from Him as well! You'll also notice that the scripture says "by the iniquity of thy traffick." To better understand this, we have to research the word "iniquity."

The word "traffick" means to travel for trading, spice or merchant, but where did Lucifer travel to? To get this answer, let's look at a few scriptures. Iniquity comes from the Hebrew word "ävon", and if we search out the word, we'll discover that it means depravity and perversity. The word "perversity" comes from the Hebrew word "avah," which means "to bend" or "to twist." According to Strong's Concordance, it also means "to crook." Another way to say this is "to make crooked." When you bend something, you have to turn it. Lucifer was turning the winds' (the breaths of God or, better yet, the spirits) attention away from God, thus, causing them to become contrary winds! He was bending their perspective of God! But, in order for Lucifer to sell a lie, he had to have a market for that lie! In other words, who was he trading to? The angels, of course! He was turning what were once "good breaths" to "bad breaths." Before we move forward, let's take a quick look at Lucifer's ministry.

The name Lucifer means "light-bearer." Without being too exhaustive, Lucifer was an archangel or, better yet, a covering cherub. This means that he was a high-ranking angel. Nevertheless, if we follow the scriptures, what we will come to see is that Lucifer desired God's glory for himself. He was covered in precious jewels, all of which were designed to absorb the light (presence) of God. He would then go and stand on a high place, where he would radiate the glory of God before the angels. The angels would then bow down and worship God, but seeing this, Lucifer decided that he wanted it all for himself. Please note that Lucifer was the gatekeeper of God's wisdom. Remember, he was covered in precious jewels, all of which were designed to absorb and radiate the light or the glory of God. Light represents revelation. This means that Lucifer knew what the other angels did not know, save Michael, who was (and is) also an archangel. Like Michael, Lucifer was a guardian of the secrets or, better yet, the administration of God. He was the anointed cherub that covered! As a matter of fact, think of the ark of the covenant. Atop it, you'll find two covering angels, both of which are encapsulated in gold. Both angels are facing one other, but they are also looking downward. Who did those angels atop the ark of the covenant represent?

- Michael
- Lucifer

Lucifer saw something that he was supposed to cover! But what did he see? Consider this—inside the ark of the covenant, there were three items:

1. **The Rod of Aaron:** This represented the resurrection of Jesus Christ.
2. **The Decalogue (Second Copy of the Law):** The second Law represented the second Covenant or the New Covenant.
3. **The Golden Pot of Manna:** This represented the indwelling of the Holy Spirit.

1 Peter 1:8-12
Whom having not seen, ye love; in whom, though now ye see him not, yet believing, ye rejoice with joy unspeakable and full of glory: Receiving the end of your faith, even the salvation of your souls. Of which salvation the prophets have inquired and searched diligently, who prophesied of the grace that should come unto you: Searching what, or what manner of time the Spirit of Christ which was in them did signify, when it testified beforehand the sufferings of Christ, and the glory that should follow. Unto whom it was revealed, that not unto themselves, but unto us they did minister the things, which are now reported unto you by them that have preached the gospel unto you with the Holy Ghost sent down from heaven; which things the angels desire to look into.

Exodus 37:6-9
And he made the mercy seat of pure gold: two cubits and a half was the length thereof, and one cubit and a half the breadth thereof. And he made two cherubims of gold, beaten out of one piece made he them, on the two ends of the mercy seat; one cherub on the end on this side, and another cherub on the other end on that side: out of the mercy seat made he the cherubims on the two ends thereof. And the cherubims spread out their wings on high, and covered with their wings over the mercy seat, with their faces one to another; even to the

<u>mercy seatward</u> were the faces of the cherubims.

The cherubs weren't just looking at each other, they were looking downward. They were looking into the glory of God, into the presence of God, and the ark of the covenant also represented the mind of God. In the mind of God, God hid the church, salvation and the baptism of the Holy Spirit. But He covered His revelation with angels!

One day, Lucifer looked into the glory of God and saw something that offended him. He saw the development of mankind. Why would God create a man from dust and give him so much dominion?! Why was He not giving this power and real estate to Lucifer?! Upset, Lucifer then took as many angels as he could gather to a place where he believed that God wouldn't see them. He took them into utter darkness! Remember, darkness is nothing but space that has not been occupied by God, and it goes without saying that Lucifer was completely aware of this uncharted territory. There, he began to uncover what he had been designed to cover! There, he began to twist the truth because had he told the angels the whole truth, they would not have turned away from God. Lucifer saw the darkness as prime real estate, after all, he was God's light-bearer.

Isaiah 14:12-15

How art thou fallen from heaven, O Lucifer, son of the morning! How art thou cut down to the ground, which didst weaken the nations! For thou hast said in thine heart, I will ascend into heaven, I will exalt my throne above the stars of God: I will sit also upon the mount of the congregation, in the sides of the north: I will ascend above the heights of the clouds; I will be like the most High. Yet thou shalt be brought down to hell, to the sides of the pit.

What or, better yet, who were the stars of God? The angels, of course! Lucifer desired to create a kingdom for himself, but what he didn't realize was that the glory he had which radiated in the darkness belonged to God. In other words, he would be cast into utter darkness, but he would not have the light (glory, power, love) of God to help him to navigate his new kingdom. Disconnected from God, he would become dark (dull, impotent, hateful); separated from God, he would become the very opposite of who God is! The more he escaped to the darkness, the darker he became; that is, until he could no longer radiate the glory of God. Before long, Michael felt a contrary wind! Lucifer who had once been walking with him was now facing him, meaning, he was moving contrary to the will of God. Amos 3:3 reminds us, "Can two walk together except they be agreed?"

Revelation 12:3-4

And there appeared another wonder in heaven; and behold a great red dragon, having seven heads and ten horns, and seven crowns upon his heads. And his tail drew the third part of the stars of heaven, and did cast them to the earth: and the dragon stood before the woman which was ready to be delivered, for to devour her child as soon as it was born.

Get this—in the darkness, Lucifer may have still looked the same to the angels that he deceived, but when he stepped into the light, he looked like the very thing he'd become—the adversary!

Revelation 12:7-9

And there was war in heaven: Michael and his angels fought against the dragon; and the dragon fought and his angels, and prevailed not; neither was their place found any more in heaven. And the great dragon was cast out, that old serpent, called the Devil, and Satan, which deceiveth the whole world: he was cast out into the earth, and his angels were cast out with him.

And of course, the third part of the stars are angels. Lucifer deceived and caused the fall of one-third of God's angels through his perverting or twisting of the truth! And God planned to do something with the darkness. Let's revisit Genesis 1:1-2, which reads, "In the beginning God created the heaven and the earth. And the earth was without form, and void; and darkness was upon the face of the deep. And the Spirit of God moved upon the face of the waters." God was developing the Earth for mankind! But Lucifer wanted it for himself, but he'd never get it if he was truthful. He had to invent another language or another doctrine to spew out to the angels. This is why he is called the father (source, inventor) of all lies. In this, Lucifer became Satan; he became a bad breath. When he became a bad breath or a contrary wind, he began to move against God's plans and His angels; this is what started the war.

Nowadays, there are three kingdoms:

- **The Kingdom of God**
- **The Kingdom of Man**
- **The Kingdom of Darkness**

Satan is not the "king" of the kingdom of darkness; instead, he is a ruler. When mankind fell, they went under his dominion, so anytime a person gets saved, Satan loses another citizen.

And the last part of this (already won) battle will be returning the real estate of the Earth back to mankind. John 12:30-32 reads, "Jesus answered and said, This voice came not because of me, but for your sakes. Now is the judgment of this world: now shall the prince of this world be cast out. And I, if I be lifted up from the earth, will draw all men unto me." The kingdom of man, while it belongs to God is a sub-kingdom, meaning, it is subject to one of the spiritual kingdoms. While we have domain (dominion) over the darkness, those who are still in the darkness are sublets of the kingdom of darkness.

Psalm 18:6-15
In my distress I called upon the LORD, and cried unto my God: he heard my voice out of his temple, and my cry came before him, even into his ears. Then the earth shook and trembled; the foundations also of the hills moved and were shaken, because he was wroth. There went up a smoke out of his nostrils, and fire out of his mouth devoured: coals were kindled by it. He bowed the heavens also, and came down: and darkness was under his feet. And he rode upon a cherub, and did fly: yea, he did fly upon the wings of the wind. He made darkness his secret place; his pavilion round about him were dark waters and thick clouds of the skies. At the brightness that was before him his thick clouds passed, hail stones and coals of fire. The LORD also thundered in the heavens, and the Highest gave his voice; hail stones and coals of fire. Yea, he sent out his arrows, and scattered them; and he shot out lightnings, and discomfited them. Then the channels of waters were seen, and the foundations of the world were discovered at thy rebuke, O LORD, at the blast of the breath of thy nostrils.

MEDITATION MOMENT

Psalm 24
The LORD is my shepherd; I shall not want.
He maketh me to lie down in green pastures: he leadeth me beside the still waters.
He restoreth my soul: he leadeth me in the paths of righteousness for his name's sake.
Yea, though I walk through the valley of the shadow of death, I will fear no evil: for thou art with me; thy rod and thy staff they comfort me.
Thou preparest a table before me in the presence of mine enemies: thou anointest my head with oil; my cup runneth over.
Surely goodness and mercy shall follow me all the days of my life: and I will dwell in the house of the LORD for ever.

What are the meditation points for you? List them below.

Meditation Points	
1	
2	
3	
4	
5	
6	
7	
8	
9	
10	
11	
12	
13	
14	
15	

WORD STUDY

Word	

Definition or Etymology

Word	

Definition or Etymology

Word	

Definition or Etymology

LET'S REFLECT!

What did you learn from the previous chapter?
How do you plan to apply this knowledge to your life?

_____

_____

_____

_____

_____

_____

_____

_____

_____

_____

_____

_____

_____

_____

MY ALARM CLOCK

Using the boxes below, record the dates when you had trouble sleeping.
Did you meditate that night? Write yes or no in the box provided.

Monday	Tuesday	Wednesday	Thursday	Friday	Saturday	Sunday

UNDER THE INFLUENCE

A spirit is a breath from God. If the spirit is still connected to God, it is a good breath. If the spirit is disconnected from God, it is a bad breath. But think of the range of breath. According to Georgia Institute, "Air travels out from a normal exhaled breath roughly 1 to 1.5 meters before it becomes exceedingly diluted, and water droplets are barely detectable." One meter equals 3.280839895 feet, which means that 1.5 meters is 4.9212597975 feet, which is approximately five feet in distance. This is roughly the height of the average ten or eleven-year old. This means that our breaths don't have much reach, even though they can positively or negatively impact the people closest to us at any given moment. In other words, a breath is a low-level wind. Think about it. Most of us have blown an insect off of our arms. To the insect, our breath is a mighty rushing wind, but to a human, our breath would only serve as a minor annoyance.

We are all spirits, meaning, we are individual breaths of God. And most of us will never go beyond our communities, our families and our immediate circles, meaning, we will spend the rest of our lives as breaths. Then again, many of us will reach a greater multitude of people through ministry or through some form of expertise. The more people we reach, the more ground our breaths will cover; this is called influence. Influence is Heaven's trust. The same is true on the other end of the spectrum. Satan has people he trusts to spread his influence as well.

Kingdom of God	Kingdom of Darkness
North Winds	South Winds
$\longrightarrow$	$\longleftarrow$

The arrows above represent gusts of wind that are moving against one another. One is moving right; this represents righteousness, while the other is moving in the opposite direction; this represents opposition. Consider what happens when two strong gusts of wind meet. Storms! But before the storm hits, an event called convergence takes place. What is convergence? "Convergence: When two air masses of the same temperature collide and neither is willing to go back down, the only way to go is up. As the name implies, the two winds converge and rise together in an updraft that often leads to cloud formation" (Source: How Stuff Works/Science/How Weather Works/When Air Masses Collide/Robert Lamb).

But let's look at this a little deeper.

Term	Description
Orographic Lifting	This phenomenon occurs when an airflow encounters elevated terrains, such as mountain ranges. Like a speeding car heading toward a hill, the wind simply powers up the slope. As it rises with the topography, water vapor in the airflow condenses and forms clouds. This side of the mountain is called the windward side and typically hosts a great deal of cloud cover and precipitation. The other side of the mountain, the leeward side, is generally less lucky. The airflow loses much of its moisture in climbing the windward side. Many mountain ranges virtually squeeze incoming winds like a sponge and, as a result, their leeward sides are home to dry wastes and deserts.
Frontal Wedging	When a warm air mass and a cold air mass collide, you get a front. Remember how low-pressure warm air rises and cold high-pressure air moves into its place? The same reaction happens here, except the two forces slam into each other. The cold air forms a wedge underneath the warm air, allowing it to basically ride up into the troposphere on its back and generate rain clouds. There are four main kinds of fronts, classified by airflow momentum. In a warm front, a warm air mass moves into a cold air mass. In a cold front, the opposite occurs. In a stationary front, neither air mass advances. Think of it as two fronts bumping into each other by accident. In an occluded front, a cold front overtakes a moving warm front, like an army swarming over a fleeing enemy.
Convergence	When two air masses of the same temperature collide and neither is willing to go back down, the only way to go is up. As the name implies, the two winds converge and rise together in an updraft that often leads to cloud formation.
Localized Convective Lifting	Remember the city example? This phenomenon employs the exact same principle, except on a smaller scale. Unequal heating on the Earth's surface can cause a pocket of air to heat faster than the surrounding air. The pocket ascends, taking water vapor with it, which can form clouds. An example of this might be a rocky clearing in a field or an airport runway, as both absorb more heat than the surrounding area.

(Chart Source: HowStuffWorks.com/Science/How Weather Works/Robert Lamb)

These contrary winds can collide and form thunderstorms, tornadoes and/or hurricanes. This is similar to what happened in Heaven when two contrary winds met. Michael and Lucifer clashed, and Lucifer was cast out of Heaven, along with his angels. Now known as the ruler of darkness, Satan is still a contrary wind; he is our adversary. This means that when we work for the Kingdom of God, we by default, are (or should be) contrary winds to the kingdom of darkness.

But what about influence? Let's look up the definition of this word.
Influence:
- to affect or alter by indirect or intangible means
- to have an effect on the condition or development of

We've all heard the term "under the influence." What this means is that the person in question's normal mode of reasoning has been impaired by an external agent such as drugs or alcohol that, of course, have been consumed. However, a Christian can be under the influence of a contrary wind, just as an unbeliever is under the influence of that same wind. This is called rebellion which, the Bible tells us is as the sin of witchcraft. As a matter of fact, Apostle Paul rebuked the Church of Galatia with these words, "O foolish Galatians, who hath bewitched you, that ye should not obey the truth, before whose eyes Jesus Christ hath been evidently set forth, crucified among you?" The word "bewitched" here comes from the Greek word "baskainó", and it literally means "to slander." Isn't this what Lucifer did? He slandered the very nature and name of God to many of the angels! Other synonyms include:
- fascinate
- overpower
- to cast an evil spell

Slander (Etymology)
late 13c., "state of impaired reputation, disgrace or dishonor;" c. 1300, "a false tale; the fabrication and dissemination of false tales," from Anglo-French esclaundre, Old French esclandre "scandalous statement," alteration ("with interloping l" [Century Dictionary]) of escandle, escandre "scandal," from Latin scandalum "cause of offense, stumbling block, temptation" (see scandal). From late 14c. as "bad situation, evil action; a person causing such a state of affairs."
Source: Online Etymology Dictionary

In short, what Lucifer did was use his power and influence to bewitch one-third of God's angels. In other words, he brought them under the influence of a lie because again, had they known the truth, most (if not all) of them would not have turned away from God. This doesn't, however, render them guiltless since they all had their individual relationships with God. They could have easily done like the rest of the angels and rejected Lucifer's merchandise. They knew that they would be at enmity with God should they follow Lucifer's lead, but they were willing to take the risk, after all, Lucifer was a high-ranking angel; he was a "covering cherub." He knew things that they didn't know. He likely told them about his plans to occupy the darkness, promising them their own real estate (kingdoms) and pointing out God's plans to create mankind. "They are made of dirt! Let them worship us!" Like Eve, they considered his lies and imagined a world where they could be gods; they imagined a world where they would be worshiped. Please note that not all of the angels fell into this trap. One-third of them did, but the rest refused to betray God's trust. This means that while 33 percent of the angels that were in Heaven turned away from God, no less than 66 percent of them did not succumb to the temptation that was Lucifer. God had entrusted Lucifer with influence, but he turned and used that influence to create one of the biggest and most pronounced exoduses to ever take place. And get this—these angels had everything that they needed and wanted, but Lucifer was cunning enough to point out the one thing that they did not have, which was their own kingdoms.

Lucifer was a wind, meaning, he had (and still has) a lot of influence. He now uses this influence to create demonic doctrines designed to grow his kingdom. For example, when we begin to venture into the topics of meditation and reflection, a lot of believers get nervous. Again, this is because the New Age movement is now claiming these terms as their own. Howbeit, meditation is a Christian concept, but when believers and non-believers meditate on doctrines that are contrary to the Word of God, they fall under the influence (spell) of demons. Meditation is not a New Age concept! The question is, what are you meditating on?

Ephesians 4:11-15

And he gave some, apostles; and some, prophets; and some, evangelists; and some, pastors and teachers; for the perfecting of the saints, for the work of the ministry, for the edifying of the body of Christ: Till we all come in the unity of the faith, and of the knowledge of the Son of God, unto a perfect man, unto the measure of the stature of the fullness of Christ: That we henceforth be no more children, tossed to and fro, and carried about with **every wind of doctrine**, by the sleight of men, and cunning craftiness, whereby they lie in wait to deceive; but speaking the truth in love, may grow up into him in all things, which is the head, even Christ.

There are many doctrines out there which, of course, have all set the stage for the emergence of false religions. And we could have many discussions about these religions, their beliefs and the fact that they are false religions, but this wouldn't serve to save the billions of souls who are currently unsaved. Right now (2020), there are approximately 7.6 billion people on the face of this planet, but only 2.4 billion of these souls have accepted Jesus Christ as their Lord and Savior. This means that roughly 5.2 billion people are still in the dark. Let's look at some numbers.

- Currently, only 31.57 percent of the world's population is saved.
- The Population Reference Bureau estimates that, to date, roughly around 107 billion people have ever lived.
- It is estimated that Jesus was born around four thousand years after the creation of mankind, and it's been approximately two thousand years since His death and resurrection. Let's be nice and assume that twenty percent of the 107 billion souls to ever walk the face of this planet were saved. This would mean that 86 billion people who've ever lived were not saved before they transitioned.

Hear me—false religions gain ground when believers refuse to share the gospel! Our problem is that we like to surround ourselves with other believers, where we serve as breaths, meaning, our words have little reach, but Atheists, Satanists and pagans are acting as winds, covering as much ground as they can! For example, a witch sees a woman seated on a bus, crying and looking miserable, and the witch sees an opportunity to grow her own influence. The witch then approaches the woman, comforts her and gets her to talk about the source of her agony. All the while, a Christian is sitting right next the woman, and hadn't considered comforting her or sharing the gospel with her for one second. This is because we treat Christianity like a members-only country club where only the healed and the whole are welcome. Broken people are often seen as liabilities, so we ignore them and make them feel unwelcome and inferior; that is, until they get the hint and go find themselves a church that we believe is more suited for "their kind." When they finally do leave, we gather around people like ourselves (pompous, narcissistic and entitled) and discuss how rejected the now former member was. That former member gets on a bus, sits next to another Christian and cries about what she's just experienced at one of our churches. The neighboring Christian ignores her pain, looking around for another seat and hoping that the fallen soldier doesn't accidentally spill her tears onto her brand new Louis Vuitton bag. A few feet away, a witch notices the woman crying, so she gets out of her seat and makes her way to the back of the bus. She then hands the woman a tissue, offers her a hug, and once she's gotten her to calm down, she listens intently to the woman's story. She then gives the woman a psychic reading, and both women eventually exit the bus, heading to their respective destinations—utter darkness! Nevertheless, every believer that let that soul slip through their fingers in this story will stand around, wondering when it'll be their time to grab a mic, stand behind a podium and preach about love and revival. Hear me—if you won't use the range you have now, why would God then turn around and let you become a wind of influence when you don't even have enough love to share with your neighbor?!

Of course, it all starts with character. You have to smell your own breath before you subject others to it. What this means is, you have to develop your own character before you attempt to develop someone else's. In Matthew 7:3-5, Jesus said it this way, "And why beholdest thou the mote that is in thy brother's eye, but considerest not the beam that is in thine own eye? Or how wilt thou say to thy brother, Let me pull out the mote out of thine eye; and, behold, a beam is in thine own eye? Thou hypocrite, first cast out the beam out of thine own eye; and then shalt thou see clearly to cast out the mote out of thy brother's eye." In other words, don't talk about her rejection until you've dealt with your own. Don't talk about his abandonment issues until you've dealt with your own. Again, this simply means that the strongest winds that we'll ever have to endure will have to come from our own mouths. Think about where we are now in 2020. We now have to wear a face mask every time we leave our homes. What this has done for many of us is made us smell our own breaths. When we stand talking with people, they no longer have to be subject to our halitosis. Instead, we are the ones being humbled by our own breaths. I believe that this is prophetic within itself! We have to encourage ourselves in the Lord; we have to acknowledge and confess our sins before we start highlighting somebody else's sins. We have to change ourselves before we'll have enough power to influence change in the lives of others.

The Breakdown of Man		
Body	Soul	Spirit

1. You are a spirit
2. You possess a soul
3. You live in a body

This is important when discussing character which, of course, is a soulish issue, but your character doesn't just affect your soul, it also affects your spirit. Your body is your earthly hub; it's where your soul and spirit are both housed. Your soul, on the other hand, has three dimensions. They are:

Mind	Emotions	Will

And then, there's your spirit. It is the very breath of God within you. It's the part of you that is the most mysterious; it is your life force—spiritualists would call this your energy, but it's so much more than that. Your spirit is the part of you that makes you like God. Remember, we were created in His image. When we hear this, we often think about our physical appearances, but God is Spirit, so when the scriptures say that we are made in His image, the author is literally talking about our spirits. Think of it this way—your mind is the epicenter of your soul. It is the switchboard, the headquarters or the lighthouse of your existence. Your mind houses three systems; they are:

Your Filtering System	Your Belief System	Your Habits

Your filtering system is the immune system of your mind. It filters through the information that you have been subjected to at any given moment, and that information is then confronted by:

1. Your already established beliefs.
2. What you've been told or taught (these aren't necessarily beliefs, but this is information that you house, but have not necessarily accepted as truths or false information. This may include many of your religious beliefs, cultures, traditions, etc.).
3. Your fears.
4. Your suspicions.
5. Your plans.

If you accept the information as true, it then enters your belief system. If you believe it to be untrue, your mind expels it in one of three ways.

1. **Indifference or Offense:** This is the fever of the soul. This is when your temperature rises to combat what you've been told. This is when you may find yourself questioning, confronting or even talking about the person who brought you the information that you've now decided to be false.
2. **Laughter:** This is the sneeze of the soul. If someone says or suggests something that you deem to be ridiculous, your disagreement may manifest itself through laughter. For example, if a man walked up to you and said that Judas Iscariot appeared to him while he was taking a shower, took him to Mars and told him that he was the last prophet alive, you may find yourself laughing. What you're doing is rejecting the information, while finding the humor in it.
3. **Grief:** This is the cough of the soul. This typically happens when you've accepted something as true, but you eventually discover it to be untrue. To rid your soul of the toxins (lies), your heart will begin to expel the misinformation through a process called grief.

And finally, your beliefs open the door to your habits. Wrongful or toxic habits are called strongholds. Your habits are the reactions of your belief system. These are the things that you do habitually, and of course, your habits create your habitat. Your habitat is what we refer to as a comfort zone; it is your mindset or what you've set your mind to. Your mindset is the projector of your reality; it may not create the pictures that you see before you everyday, but it colors, highlights, adds to and takes away from those pictures.

Habit	Habitat
• a settled tendency or usual manner of behavior • an acquired mode of behavior that has become nearly or completely involuntary • a behavior pattern acquired by frequent repetition or physiologic exposure that shows itself in regularity or increased facility of performance	• the place or environment where a plant or animal naturally or normally lives and grows • the typical place of residence of a person or a group • a housing for a controlled physical environment in which people can live under surrounding inhospitable conditions

Source: Merriam Webster's Online Dictionary

Your emotions are the weather of your thinking patterns. If you are a negative person, chances are, you're always in a bad mood. So, in your world, you're always in a storm, preparing for a storm or you have simply become the storm. Think of the weather patterns in some of the United States. Florida is known for having at least 237 days of sunshine in a year, meaning, it's known to be sunny, bright and pleasant. For this reason, it is one of the top tourist destinations in the United States. New York, on the other hand, is known to be relatively colder, but it remains a top tourist destination as well because of its historical landmarks and tall buildings. Now, imagine if Florida and New York were people, and their weather patterns represented their attitudes. Who would you want to hang out with more? Most people would say Florida because it's sunny most of the year, but remember, Florida has more storms than any of the other states, so if Florida were a person, it would be an emotional person. New York would be unemotional, but consistent. However, whenever New York had a cold spell, she wouldn't speak to you for months on end, unlike Florida who would scream at you for no reason, hang up the phone in your face and then, call back 15 minutes later asking if you wanted to go to the beach. The point is, your thinking patterns set the stage for your emotions. And it goes without saying, what you believe and how you feel will both determine your will; this is the expression of your soul. Let's look at a few pictures.

BREAK DOWN OF MAN
1 Thessalonians 5:23

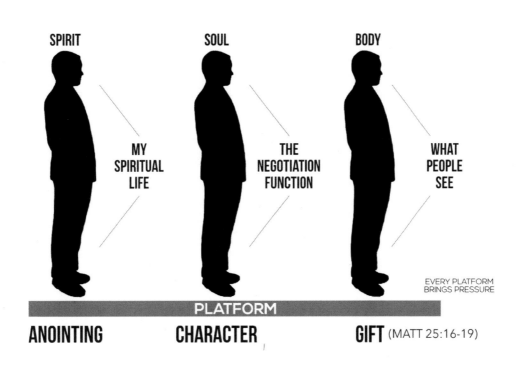

KINGDOM FUNCTION

Your body is what people see; another word for "body" is "earth-suit." We also refer to it as our flesh. Please note that the word "flesh" isn't just limited to the body, it also denotes our carnal desires. You'll notice that your body corresponds with your gift. How so? This is the part of you that you can give away (not in totality, but through the use of your will). Consider a very popular passage of scriptures, which is Romans 12:1. It reads, "I beseech you therefore, brethren, by the mercies of God, that ye present your bodies a living sacrifice, holy, acceptable unto God, which is your reasonable service." Notice the word "present" in this text. To present means "to offer." This is an act of will. You can also read it this way, "I beseech you, brethren, by the mercies of God that you present your body as a present." A present, of course, means a gift. God gave you the gift of a body, but you have to give it back to Him.

If we continue reading in Romans 12, we'll notice that verse two deals with our character. It reads, "And be not conformed to this world: but be ye transformed by the renewing of your mind, that ye may prove what is that good, and acceptable, and perfect, will of God." When the scripture deals with conformation, the author is referencing our character. Our character is the shape of our soul.

Next, there is the soul. Your soul is made up of your mind, will and emotions. Notice in the diagram above that it is seated right between your flesh and your spirit. It's more like a gradient between the two; it is the medium or mediator between your flesh and your spirit man which, of course, are at enmity with one another. This is why it's your negotiation function. Your spirit was created in the image of God; your spirit wants to sit in His presence day in and day out, but your flesh wants to be a god. Your soul mediates this brawl and will always side with the dimension of you that you feed the most. If your flesh is in the front seat, your soul will be led by your flesh; if your spirit is in the front seat, your soul will be led by your spirit. But when you allow your flesh and your spirit to alternate, your soul will then split; this is what the Bible refers to as double-mindedness. Also note that your soul corresponds with your character.

The Greek word for "character" is "charaktér," and according to Strong's Concordance, it means "a tool for engraving." Your character is the fingerprint of your soul. It's not just the impression you make on others, it's the impression you've made on yourself. Let's look a little closer at this word.

Character (HELPS Word-studies)
5481 xaraktér – properly, an engraving; (figuratively) an exact impression (likeness) which also reflects inner character. [5481 /xaraktér was originally a tool (used for engraving) and then came to mean "a die" ("mould"). Finally, it stood for a stamp or impress used on a coin or seal (see H, 368). In each case, the stamp conveyed the reality behind the image.] The Greek fathers (ad 100 -500) used 5481 /xaraktér ("the ultimate radiance") of the supreme effulgence of Christ, showing forth His glory as the second Person of the eternal Godhead (Heb 1:3).
Source: Bible Hub

Your character sets the stage for your characteristics which, of course, are the footprints of your soul. What's the difference between your character and your characteristics? Think of it this way—there are males and there are females. There are some things that men can do but women cannot do, and there are some things that women can do but men cannot do. Each person's gender is a fact, however, each gender's abilities would be the expressions of that fact. Your character is who you are or who you've become; your characteristics are the expressions of this fact. For example, if you are a positive, warm and friendly person, people would say that you're nice or you're kind. What they are doing is identifying an aspect of your character. However, the expressions of your character may manifest through you smiling at people, even when you're having a bad day; they may also manifest through you opening doors for people, hugging people, helping people or encouraging people. Your character is the shape of your soul. It is the lasting impression that you've left on others, but your characteristics are the manner in which you left those impressions.

Character	Characteristics
Fingerprint of the Soul	Footprints of the Soul
the complex of mental and ethical traits marking and often individualizing a person, group, or nation the character of the American people main or essential nature especially as strongly marked and serving to distinguish *Definition taken from Merriam-Webster*	a distinguishing trait, quality, or property a special quality or trait that makes a person, thing, or group different from others typical of a person, thing, or group: showing the special qualities or traits of a person, thing, or group *Definition taken from Merriam-Webster*

Another way to look at it is—your characteristics are the fruit of your character, but your character lies in the type of tree or plant that you are.

And finally, there is your spirit. Let's look at its etymology.

Spirit (Strong's #4151) Pneuma
from 4154; a current of air, i.e. breath (blast) or a breeze; by analogy or figuratively, a spirit, i.e. (human) the rational soul, (by implication) vital principle, mental disposition, etc., or (superhuman) an angel, demon, or (divine) God, Christ's spirit, the Holy Spirit:--ghost, life, spirit(-ual, -ually), mind. Compare 5590.
Source: Online Etymology Dictionary

The Greek word for "spirit" is "pneuma," from which we get the word "pneumonia." It if your life force; it is the part of you that's eternal. This corresponds with your anointing; it's who you really are. For example, when you're in the middle of worship, and you feel like you can cast out devils, heal the sick and perform miracles, this is who you really are! You are anointed! Think about the jewels that were in Lucifer's body. What happened to them? Remember:

1. The jewels were designed to absorb the light of God so that Lucifer could go before the angels and radiate God's glory.
2. The darkness did not and could not comprehend the light.
3. Lucifer was taking the angels in the darkness to have his illegal meetings with them,

and it was in the darkness that he slandered God's character.

Again, what happened to those jewels? Luke 39:19-20 reads, "And some of the Pharisees from among the multitude said unto him, Master, rebuke thy disciples. And he answered and said unto them, I tell you that, if these should hold their peace, the stones would immediately cry out." What or, better yet, who were the stones? People! The stones that were in Lucifer's body represented people! But when Lucifer and his angels went up against Michael and his army, Lucifer was not adorned in the jewels anymore. Instead, the book of Revelation refers to him as Satan (adversary) at this point, and he looked nothing like the beautifully radiant angel that he once was. You see, outside the will of God, something hideous began to form. Lucifer's pipes began to bend and twist until the sounds of worship that passed through them started sounding horrible. The more he stole away into the darkness, the more hideous he became; that is, until one day, he could no longer hide behind his beauty. He started looking like the monster that he is! Did the stones fall away? Possibly! But consider this—could it be that when God said to Lucifer, " Thou hast defiled thy sanctuaries by the multitude of thine iniquities, by the iniquity of thy traffick," what Lucifer had been trafficking were the jewels (people) he had been charged to bring God glory with? Is it possible that he exchanged these jewels for many of the angels' loyalties? Let's consider for a moment that Lucifer had possibly been giving charge over mankind, and just like Jesus redeemed us with His body (and blood), Lucifer had sold us through his body. Wouldn't this explain why he is considered the prince of this world? It's just a theory, but this would explain why Jesus said that we have been "bought with a price," meaning He stepped into an earth-suit (one of the jewels), began to glorify God with it, and then He drew all the brightness that had been in the trafficked jewels to Himself so that He could return the glory to God! He said, "If I be lifted up (glorified), I will draw all men unto me." And just like that, many of the demons who possessed jewels (people) watched in horror as the radiance from the jewels they had suddenly became duller and duller until the jewels became worthless. This (possibly) could have been because energy is neither created nor destroyed, it can only be transformed or transferred from one form to another. Again, science will back the scriptures if it's used properly!

Transferred	Transformed
Colossians 1:13-14	2 Corinthians 3:18
Who hath delivered us from the power of darkness, and hath translated us into the kingdom of his dear Son: In whom we have redemption through his blood, even the forgiveness of sins.	But we all, with open face beholding as in a glass the glory of the Lord, are changed into the same image from glory to glory, even as by the Spirit of the Lord.

Again, you are a spirit. You are the breath and the glory of God, and while you were in darkness (because Lucifer took you there), you have now been translated or transferred to the Kingdom of God through His Son, Christ Yeshua. This truth should change how you view Genesis 1:3-4, which reads, "And God said, Let there be light: and there was light. And God saw the light, that it was good: and God divided the light from the darkness."

Dispelling False Light

The ability for your anointing to stand upright, your character to stand upright and for your gift to stand upright is called faith. Romans 4:23 warns us this way, "For whatever does not proceed from faith is sin." The Greek word for "sin" is "harmatia," and it literally means "to miss the mark." Genesis 15:6 tells us that Abraham believed God and it was accounted or credited to him as righteousness.

Right	Upright	Righteous

Consider the word "upright." If one of your parents, guardians or teachers had said to you, "Stand up right," you would understand it to mean that, while you're standing on your feet, your shoulders are not pulled back, your spine needs to be straightened out and your legs are not locked. To stand up right would mean that there is no bend in your back (spine). All the same, to be upright means that there is no bend (perversion) in your spine (structure). Howbeit, anytime you doubt God, you miss the mark; this is what the scriptures refer to as sin.

Remember, we live in the body, we possess a soul and we are a spirit. A man's body, of course, is his legal suit; it's what legalizes his existence in the natural realm. Anything that enters the natural without an earth suit is illegal. This is why Jesus had to be born in the flesh of a human. Remember, there are three kingdoms. Let's see how they relate to each dimension of who we are.

Kingdoms	Dimensions of a Man	Parallel	Levels	Scripture
Kingdom of God	Spirit	Mind	100 Fold	Proverbs 20:27
Kingdom of Man	Soul	Will	60 Fold	Genesis 2:7
Kingdom of Darkness	Body	Emotions	30 Fold	1 Corinthians 15:50

Matthew 6:22 says, "The light of the body is the eye: if therefore thine eye be single, thy whole body shall be full of light." Amazingly enough, the New Age movement uses scripture to

substantiate their beliefs, including Matthew 6:22. They use this to establish or promote their beliefs in what they call the third eye. The concept of the third eye is directly connected to clairvoyance which Google's Online dictionary defines as, "The supposed faculty of perceiving things or events in the future or beyond normal sensory contact." Hear me—if a vision of the future comes through a person from any other spirit than the Holy Spirit, you should reject the vision! Amos 3:7 warns us this way; it reads, "Surely the Lord GOD will do nothing, but he revealeth his secret unto his servants the prophets." What can we take from this?

1. Before God does anything in the realm of the Earth, He will reveal what He's about to do to His prophets, not the prophets of Baal or any other false prophets. A witch, a warlock, a sorcerer and every other medium who taps into the spirit realm without the legality of the Holy Spirit is an illegal and ungodly source of information! They are directly connected to the kingdom of darkness, and as such, what you extract from them will be demonic. In other words, it's coming from fallen angels.

2. God has secrets! Remember, Lucifer was able to peer into the mysteries of God, and it was there that he saw something that he wanted for himself!

3. There are true, God-established prophets who are not serving God, but He only reveals His secrets to His servants. Hear me—holding the office of the prophet does not guarantee (or entitle) you to the mysteries of the Kingdom of God. It's your faithful service that gets God's attention.

And get this—there is no "third-eye awakening!" At least, not with God's people! A believer's ability to tap into the realm of the spirit is through the use of the Holy Spirit! He is not a third eye. He is the Spirit of God! Again, Matthew 6:22 deals with the light of the body, which we've come to learn is the Holy Spirit. If your eye is single, meaning, you focus on God and all that He is, your entire body will be filled with His presence! But this is no easy task! We are distracted by everything around us; in the natural, this is similar to what we call peripheral vision. This allows us to see objects and movements all around us without turning our heads, and while this can be a life-saving ability, it also serves as a tool of distraction. But tunnel vision, while a real medical condition, is often used to describe a person who's goal-oriented and focused! But in the medical world, tunnel vision is a medical condition of the eyes that causes the person who has it to see objects as if they were viewing them through a straw or a tunnel. In other words, they can only see straight up ahead; everything else around them is a blur. This is what I call the camera-effect. A high-resolution, quality camera tends to blur out the background to increase the sharpness of whatever image you point it towards. This gives the image more clarity and depth. The point of this is, information enters the body through the soul. While the body is what others see, it is just a suit, an outfit or, better yet, a covering. But all information enters the body through the soul, and all information that enters the soul enters through the natural eyes or the imagination. Let me explain.

What you see is brought into your mind and processed. If you see a squirrel, your eyes will transmit the information to your mind, where your memory bank will respond with the word "squirrel." This is because you've seen squirrels before. But what comes into your imagination will come from either of the three kingdoms.

Kingdom of God	Kingdom of Man	Kingdom of Darkness

If it comes from the Kingdom of God, it is one of the following:

Word of Wisdom	Word of Knowledge	Faith
Gifts of Healing	Working of Miracles	Prophecy
Discerning of Spirits	Diverse Tongues	Interpretation of Tongues

1 Corinthians 12:4-11 read, "Now there are diversities of gifts, but the same Spirit. And there are differences of administrations, but the same Lord. And there are diversities of operations, but it is the same God which worketh all in all. But the manifestation of the Spirit is given to every man to profit withal. For to one is given by the Spirit the word of wisdom; to another the word of knowledge by the same Spirit; to another faith by the same Spirit; to another the gifts of healing by the same Spirit; to another the working of miracles; to another prophecy; to another discerning of spirits; to another divers kinds of tongues; to another the interpretation of tongues: But all these worketh that one and the selfsame Spirit, dividing to every man severally as he will." Again, we are connected to the Holy Spirit! He is our source of information, especially information regarding the spirit realm. He communicates with our spirit and our spirit communicates with our soul. The kingdom of darkness, on the other hand, communicates with our soul by using our imaginations, the media and people; this is because Satan has absolutely no access to or contact with our spirits! This is how you know that the "third eye" concept is not only false doctrine, but it is demonic! It encourages people to process information through their own abilities without the use, guidance or aid of the Holy Spirit! So, while some people do have supernatural, superhuman abilities, the question is, "Who is the source of their power?!" And hear me—some people have supernatural insight that has been given to them by God, after all, the gifts and callings are without repentance, but when they don't accept Jesus Christ as their Lord and Savior and submit those abilities to God to be tested and filtered, they will tap into what the Bible refers to as "Satan disguising himself as an angel of light!" It is difficult to convince a prophetic person that he or she is not hearing from God when that gifting hasn't been purified or trained! So, they loan themselves to the kingdom of darkness to be used as lamps by angels (demons) who have no light left to guide them! Hear me; consider this concept—people without the Holy Spirit aren't being awakened; they

aren't getting a better consciousness of who they are! Instead, the third eye is really Satan's angels' abilities to see the world through the eyes of those who they possess! In other words, they are creatures of darkness; they are blind apparitions condemned to darkness, and people are nothing but their eyeglasses. What they are doing is trafficking knowledge, both true and false, to the natural world in exchange for a body to see through! So, New Age believers aren't being "enlightened," they are being trafficked! "But the path of the just is as the shining light, that shineth more and more unto the perfect day. The way of the wicked is as darkness: they know not at what they stumble" (Proverbs 4:18-19). And please note that by the word "wicked," the Bible isn't necessarily saying that unbelievers are murderers, rapists and extortioners! It simply means "unholy, unregenerate, ungodly." What this means is that "good people," by our earthly standards, can be and often are considered wicked by God because they are without Him, and He alone is holy!

- **Proverbs 21:2:** Every way of a man is right in his own eyes: but the LORD pondereth the hearts.
- **Proverbs 3:5:** Trust in the LORD with all thine heart; and lean not unto thine own understanding.
- **Proverbs 14:12:** There is a way which seemeth right unto a man, but the end thereof are the ways of death.

What is false light? Simply put, it's false doctrine. It gives a person false knowledge, a false sense of security and a religion without God. It is Satan's attempt to retake his position and role as Lucifer.

Satan	Lucifer
Means "adversary" or "enemy of God."	Means "light bearer" or "shining one."

Lucifer lost his radiance. He no longer has access to the glory of God. Howbeit, we are all little lights, so he's drawn to us, but not in a good way. He wants to steal our light because he has no light of his own to source from. The point is, there is no true light and there are no open eyes outside of YAHWEH. Everything outside of the Kingdom is false! This is why God said, "Let God be true and every man a liar!" We are not good in and of ourselves! Jesus traded places with us on the cross, and now we are lights shining in the darkness!

The Fall of Man				
Creation	**Temptation**	**Fall**	**Punishment**	**Salvation**
(Genesis 2:7)	(Genesis 1:3-7)	(Genesis 3:6-7)	(Genesis 3:16-19)	(John 3:16-17)
And the LORD	Now the serpent	And when the	Unto the woman	For God so loved

Creation (Genesis 2:7)	Temptation (Genesis 1:3-7)	Fall (Genesis 3:6-7)	Punishment (Genesis 3:16-19)	Salvation (John 3:16-17)
God formed man of the dust of the ground, and breathed into his nostrils the breath of life; and man became a living soul.	was more subtil than any beast of the field which the LORD God had made. And he said unto the woman, Yea, hath God said, Ye shall not eat of every tree of the garden? And the woman said unto the serpent, We may eat of the fruit of the trees of the garden: But of the fruit of the tree which is in the midst of the garden, God hath said, Ye shall not eat of it, neither shall ye touch it, lest ye die. And the serpent said unto the woman, Ye shall not surely die: For God doth know that in the day ye eat thereof, then your eyes shall be opened, and ye shall be as gods, knowing	woman saw that the tree was good for food, and that it was pleasant to the eyes, and a tree to be desired to make one wise, she took of the fruit thereof, and did eat, and gave also unto her husband with her; and he did eat. And the eyes of them both were opened, and they knew that they were naked; and they sewed fig leaves together, and made themselves aprons.	he said, I will greatly multiply thy sorrow and thy conception; in sorrow thou shalt bring forth children; and thy desire shall be to thy husband, and he shall rule over thee. And unto Adam he said, Because thou hast hearkened unto the voice of thy wife, and hast eaten of the tree, of which I commanded thee, saying, Thou shalt not eat of it: cursed is the ground for thy sake; in sorrow shalt thou eat of it all the days of thy life; thorns also and thistles shall it bring forth to thee; and thou shalt eat the herb of the field; in the sweat of thy face shalt thou eat bread, till thou	the world, that he gave his only begotten Son, that whosoever believeth in him should not perish, but have everlasting life. For God sent not his Son into the world to condemn the world; but that the world through him might be saved.

Creation (Genesis 2:7)	Temptation (Genesis 1:3-7)	Fall (Genesis 3:6-7)	Punishment (Genesis 3:16-19)	Salvation (John 3:16-17)
	good and evil.		return unto the ground; for out of it wast thou taken: for dust thou art, and unto dust shalt thou return.	

Man became a "living" soul.

Living or Live (Etymology)
c. 1200, "alive, not dead," also "residing, staying," present-participle adjective from live (v.)). Replaced Old English lifende "living, having life." Of water, "constantly flowing," late 14c., a biblical idiom. Of rock, stone, etc., "in its original state and place," from Latin use of vivus in reference to unwrought stone. Living dead was used from early 18c. in various figurative senses ("those who though dead live in their writings," etc.), from 1919 in reference to those who have died and been revived. From 1971 in reference to zombies, vampires, etc.
Source: Online Etymology Dictionary

First and foremost, as you search the scriptures, you'll notice that Adam and Eve were referred to as "man." Adam was a man; Eve was a woman (man with a womb). After the fall, they became mankind or, better yet, a hybrid or watered down version of what God had initially created. Another word for "mankind" is "human." The prefix "hum" means "ground." The word "human" means "fallen man" or "humbled man." We are a kind of man, but not necessarily God's original design. This, of course, is because of our sin nature.

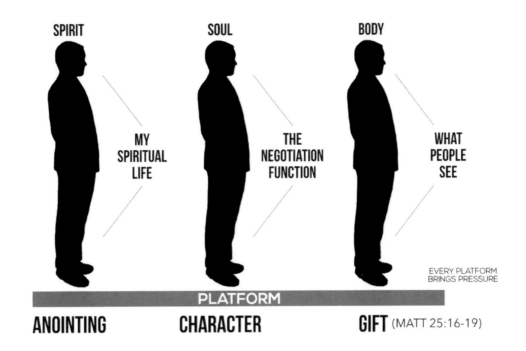

KINGDOM FUNCTION

BREAK DOWN OF MAN
1 Thessalonians 5:23

SPIRIT

SOUL

BODY

MY
SPIRITUAL
LIFE

THE
NEGOTIATION
FUNCTION

WHAT
PEOPLE
SEE

EVERY PLATFORM
BRINGS PRESSURE

PLATFORM

ANOINTING

CHARACTER

GIFT (MATT 25:16-19)

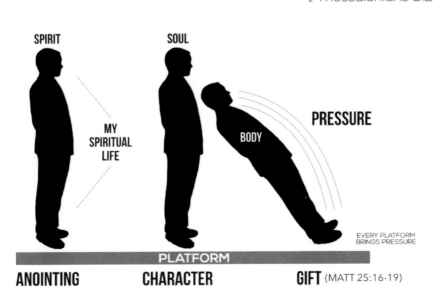

BREAK DOWN OF MAN
1 Thessalonians 5:23

KINGDOM FUNCTION

SPIRIT

SOUL

MY
SPIRITUAL
LIFE

BODY

PRESSURE

EVERY PLATFORM
BRINGS PRESSURE

PLATFORM

ANOINTING

CHARACTER

GIFT (MATT 25:16-19)

When man was first created, like God, he was (and still is) divided into three parts: spirit, soul and body. You'll notice in this diagram that his spirit was on the forefront. He was led by his spirit; he walked by faith and not by sight. As a matter of fact, the glory of God was so thick and tangible that neither Adam nor Eve realized they were naked. But after they fell, their eyes were opened, and the glory lifted from them. Genesis 3:6-7 reads, "And when the woman saw that the tree was good for food, and that it was pleasant to the eyes, and a tree to be desired to make one wise, she took of the fruit thereof, and did eat, and gave also unto her husband with her; and he did eat. And the eyes of them both were opened, and they knew that they were naked; and they sewed fig leaves together, and made themselves aprons." Understand this—when their eyes opened in the natural, their spiritual eyes closed. (This was not a "third eye"! Adam and Eve's spiritual eyes closed because they lost the Holy Spirit, and outside of Him, man is spiritually blind. The only way for us to receive the Holy Spirit is through Christ, so every other attempt to access the spirit realm outside of Him is both illegal and demonic!) In other words, their spirits took the backseat and their flesh was thrust into the front seat. They would now be led by their flesh. The soul, on the other hand, would now have to adjust to another leader—one that had been perverted or twisted by sin in the same manner that Lucifer's organs (pipes and timbrels) had been twisted when he'd sinned against God.

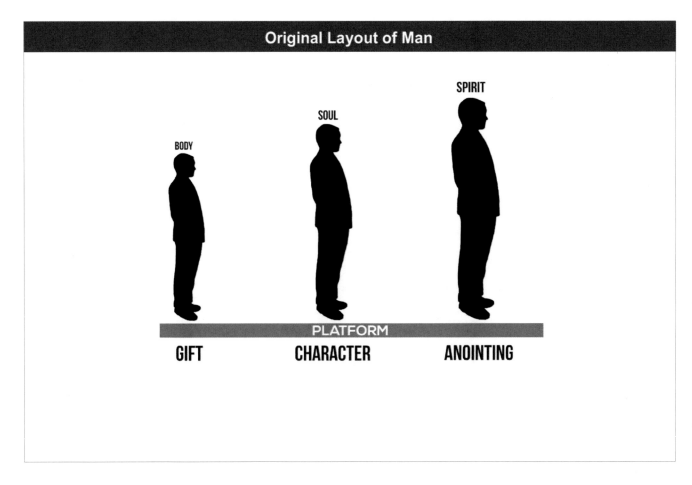

46

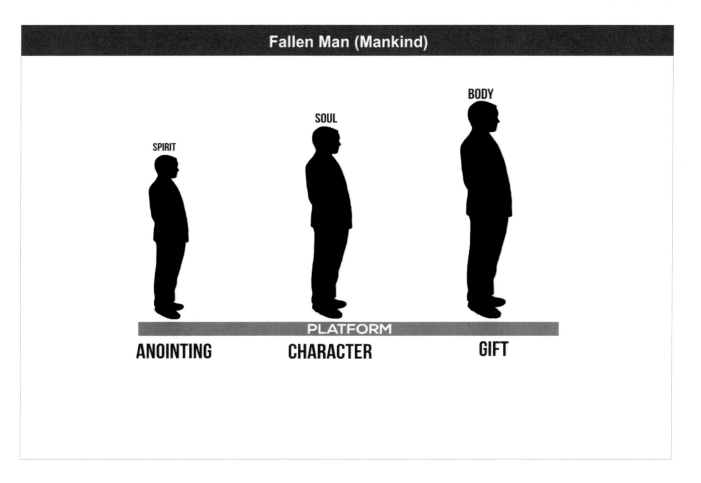

In the above diagram, you can now see mankind's new layout. In the original design, man was led by his spirit, but after he fell, mankind started being led by his flesh. He would now need to till the ground that was his flesh so that he could bring forward spiritual fruits. And this would be an impossible task; that is, until the birth, death and resurrection of Christ Jesus. And hear me—after the fall, man wouldn't just hear the winds, he would feel them. This is called lust! Lust isn't limited to sexual desires; lust is any ungodly, unbridled desire of the flesh that goes against the ordinance of God. These are the pressures that we feel on a daily basis! For every level we step into or onto, there are different types of pressure that we must endure. Think about climbing a mountain. Air pressure decreases as altitude increases, so the pressure at the top is more bearable than the pressures at the bottom. However, the man who ascends the mountain is not free from pressure, not even by a long shot! You see, he now has to deal with the high winds, coupled with the thin air which makes it difficult for him to breathe. Science Line reported the following:

> "With so much less oxygen, your body has to breathe more to get the same amount of the essential molecule. This leads to the shortness of breath, dizziness and tiredness indicative of altitude sickness. The oxygen drop combined with the decreased air pressure packs a one-two punch to your cardiovascular system. In order for your lungs to breathe air in without duress, the pressure has to be higher outside your body. But at

high altitudes, the outside air pressure is lower than it is inside your lungs, making it more difficult to pull in the thinner air and for your veins to pump oxygen throughout the body. As a result, heart rate and blood pressure skyrocket as your body kicks into overdrive. This can lead to more unpleasant symptoms, including headache and confusion."
(Source: Science Line/Why do you feel so awful at high altitudes?/Rebecca Harrington)

So, as you can see, while you may no longer have to deal with the atmospheric pressures produced by downward traveling winds, you now have to deal with the pressures that come from within. A multimillionaire or billionaire is hardly moved by the opinions of people, but he has to deal with the pressures associated with wealth! Everyone wants to sue him, many of the people in his circle envy him, and because of the love of money, he has to go above and beyond the call of duty to protect his family and his assets! One wrong decision could cost him his life, his family or his lifestyle. He can't walk around in the mall parking lot openly. He deals with a different type of pressure; all too often that pressure is suspicion!

Every platform comes with pressure. Pressure is like gravity; it will push you in one direction or the other. But these pressures come from winds. Again, most of these winds represent the words of naysayers; this is low-level pressure. Next, there's the pressure put on the mind by worry, doubt and fear, and finally, there's spiritual pressure. These pressures come from demon-bound people! This is why God established the five-fold ministry! Ephesians 4:11-14 reads, "And he gave some, apostles; and some, prophets; and some, evangelists; and some, pastors and teachers; for the perfecting of the saints, for the work of the ministry, for the edifying of the body of Christ: Till we all come in the unity of the faith, and of the knowledge of the Son of God, unto a perfect man, unto the measure of the stature of the fullness of Christ: That we henceforth be no more children, **tossed to and fro, and carried about with every wind of doctrine**, by the sleight of men, and cunning craftiness, whereby they lie in wait to deceive." Notice here that Apostle Paul said that the purpose of the five-fold gifts were to perfect (mature) believers. Why? So, we wouldn't be tossed to and fro (double-minded) by every wind of doctrine. In summary, so we wouldn't be led astray by demonic people. This is where it gets interesting! He said the winds of doctrine came by the sleight of men! That word "sleight" simply means "cunning" or "craftiness." In other words, the pressures come from the many voices out there who say, "We represent the true religion! Follow us if you want to be saved!" To prevent us from falling into the many snares that we've witnessed some of our loved ones fall into, God anointed and deployed five-fold ministerial leaders to encourage, edify (educate) and exhort the body of Christ.

Again, every platform brings pressure, and if you're led by your flesh, the pressure you feel will come through your flesh. This is why the scriptures tell us to be led by the Spirit! You see, once you were filled with the Spirit of God, your spirit was reconciled with His!

Galatians 5:18	Romans 8:14	Matthew 4:1
But if ye be led of the Spirit, ye are not under the law.	For as many as are led by the Spirit of God, they are the sons of God.	Then was Jesus led up of the Spirit into the wilderness to be tempted of the devil.

If you're led by the flesh, on the other hand, you'll deal with the many pressures, winds and temptations that come out of the kingdom of darkness. Consider the temptations that Christ endured.

Matthew 4:1-11
Then was Jesus led up of the Spirit into the wilderness to be tempted of the devil. And when he had fasted forty days and forty nights, he was afterward an hungred. And when the tempter came to him, he said, If thou be the Son of God, command that these stones be made bread. But he answered and said, It is written, Man shall not live by bread alone, but by every word that proceedeth out of the mouth of God. Then the devil taketh him up into the holy city, and setteth him on a pinnacle of the temple, and saith unto him, If thou be the Son of God, cast thyself down: for it is written, He shall give his angels charge concerning thee: and in their hands they shall bear thee up, lest at any time thou dash thy foot against a stone. Jesus said unto him, It is written again, Thou shalt not tempt the Lord thy God. Again, the devil taketh him up into an exceeding high mountain, and sheweth him all the kingdoms of the world, and the glory of them; and saith unto him, All these things will I give thee, if thou wilt fall down and worship me. Then saith Jesus unto him, Get thee hence, Satan: for it is written, Thou shalt worship the Lord thy God, and him only shalt thou serve. Then the devil leaveth him, and, behold, angels came and ministered unto him.

Jesus was tempted in all three dimensions: body, soul and spirit!

Body	Soul	Spirit
And when he had fasted forty days and forty nights, he was afterward an hungred. And when the tempter came to him, he said, If thou be the	Then the devil taketh him up into the holy city, and setteth him on a pinnacle of the temple, and saith unto him, If thou be the Son of God, cast	Again, the devil taketh him up into an exceeding high mountain, and sheweth him all the kingdoms of the world, and the glory of them; and

Body	Soul	Spirit
Son of God, command that these stones be made bread.	thyself down: for it is written, He shall give his angels charge concerning thee: and in their hands they shall bear thee up, lest at any time thou dash thy foot against a stone.	saith unto him, All these things will I give thee, if thou wilt fall down and worship me.

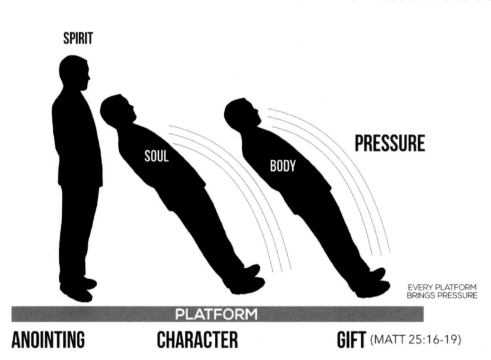

KINGDOM FUNCTION

BREAK DOWN OF MAN
1 Thessalonians 5:23

SPIRIT

SOUL

BODY

PRESSURE

EVERY PLATFORM BRINGS PRESSURE

PLATFORM

ANOINTING   CHARACTER   GIFT (MATT 25:16-19)

This is because the Lord had not yet been glorified, so Satan had to tempt His flesh. Jesus faced the many pressures so that we could see that not only can we overcome the temptations of the enemy, but He demonstrated to us how to overcome those temptations. Hebrews 4:15 says it this way, "For we have not an high priest which cannot be touched with the feeling of our infirmities; but was in all points tempted like as we are, yet without sin." Jesus had been tempted too! Nevertheless, even after witnessing the Lord overcome temptation, we still fall into its many snares when we are led by our flesh. Notice in the above diagram that the body of the man has fallen; this is due to the many winds and pressures associated with being human. Maybe he fell into lust, maybe he has a gambling problem or maybe he has anger issues; either way, you'll notice that when his body falls, it directly impacts his soul. What is the soul? The mind, will and emotions. The pressures that come against an impacted soul are called guilt, shame and regret! And these three are more than just feelings. They can directly impact our mental health or leave us in need of deliverance! In other words, it can easily go from being a lust issue to a spiritual one!

This is what sin does to the man. It inevitably wears him down until nothing is standing but his spirit, and eventually, even his spirit can be broken. Proverbs 18:14 says it this way, "The spirit of a man will sustain his infirmity; but a wounded spirit who can bear?" What is a broken spirit? Depression! Hear me—when we fail, when we fall or when we start dealing with issues in our minds or bodies, it is our spirit-man who encourages us, but if we don't correct, not just the behavior, but address our way of thinking, it is only a matter of time before we start wrestling with a broken spirit. This is what happened to Elijah after he allowed Jezebel's threats to push him towards the edge of his sanity! And get this, it wasn't her threats that made him want to commit suicide! Let's look at the story!

1 Kings 19:1-4
And Ahab told Jezebel all that Elijah had done, and withal how he had slain all the prophets with the sword. Then Jezebel sent a messenger unto Elijah, saying, So let the gods do to me, and more also, if I make not thy life as the life of one of them by to morrow about this time. And when he saw that, he arose, and went for his life, and came to Beersheba, which belongeth to Judah, and left his servant there. But he himself went a day's journey into the wilderness, and came and sat down under a juniper tree: and he requested for himself that he might die; and said, It is enough; now, O LORD, take away my life; for I am not better than my fathers.

Elijah didn't ask the Lord to kill him just because Jezebel had threatened his life! He dealt with the very pressures that most prophets and prophetic people deal with whenever they believe they've failed; they are guilt and shame! Elijah had run away because of fear; this was a soulish issue, but guilt and shame started wearing down on his spirit! This is what the Bible refers to as a troubled or vexed spirit. Remember, your spirit is the breath of God. This is why James 4:14 states, "Whereas ye know not what shall be on the morrow. For what is your life? It is even a vapor, that appeareth for a little time, and then vanisheth away."

Measuring and Managing Influence		
Body	**Soul**	**Spirit**
What People See	The Negotiation Function	My Spiritual Life
Gift	Character	Anointing

The same way we are body, soul and spirit, we are gift, character and anointing. Your gift corresponds with your body, your character corresponds with your soul and your anointing corresponds with your spirit. Remember, you live in a body, you possess a soul and you are a spirit. Let's say it another way—you live in a gift, you possess character and you are an anointing! Your anointing is who you really are. This is why God warned us all when He said, "Touch not my anointed and do my prophets no harm." Why did God use the word "touch"? Think about anointing oil. Traditionally, when a man was anointed by God to serve as king over Israel, God would send a prophet to anoint that man with oil. The pouring of oil in the natural was symbolic of God's Spirit being poured out upon that man. Remember, in 1 Samuel 16, God sent the Prophet Samuel to anoint David as king over Israel. Once the deed was finished, the scriptures tell us that the Spirit of the Lord came upon David in power. "Touch not mine anointed." In this, God simply means do not approach what is sacred in a casual way or, better yet, don't touch, lead astray (seduce) or captivate anything or anyone He's set aside for His use. Think about the story of Uzzah.

2 Samuel 6:5-8
And David and all the house of Israel were celebrating before the Lord, with songs and lyres and harps and tambourines and castanets and cymbals. And when they came to the threshing floor of Nacon, Uzzah put out his hand to the ark of God and took hold of it, for the oxen stumbled. And the anger of the Lord was kindled against Uzzah, and God struck him down there because of his error, and he died there beside the ark of God.

Again, what was in the ark of the covenant?

The Rod of Aaron	The Decalogue	The Golden Pot of Manna
This represented the resurrection of Jesus Christ.	The second Law represented the second Covenant or the New Covenant.	This represented the indwelling of the Holy Spirit.

This takes us back to the moment when God cast mankind out of the Garden of Eden. Genesis 3:24 (ESV) reads, "He drove out the man, and at the east of the garden of Eden he placed the cherubim and a flaming sword that turned every way to guard the way to the tree of life." Remember, Jesus is the Tree of Life. The cherubim atop the ark of the covenant represent the angels who were once entrusted to look into the glory of God—Michael and Lucifer. Of course, Lucifer fell, so he was cast out of God's presence. Lucifer's crime was that he became too familiar or casual with God. This behavior not only breeds rebellion, it breeds envy, competition and comparison. And when Lucifer fell into these snares, he took one-third of God's angels with him. In Leviticus, two of Aaron's sons died because of how they approached the presence of God. Leviticus 10:1-3 reads, "And Nadab and Abihu, the sons of Aaron, took either of them his censer, and put fire therein, and put incense thereon, and offered strange fire before the LORD, which he commanded them not. And there went out fire from the LORD, and devoured them, and they died before the LORD. Then Moses said unto Aaron, This is it that the LORD spake, saying, I will be sanctified in them that come nigh me, and before all the people I will be glorified. And Aaron held his peace." In other words, we cannot share in God's glory. Anytime mere men approach God the wrong way, it's because they are puffed up with pride and rebellion. Hear me—the ark of God was sacred; it represented the manifested presence of God. Then and now, you could not and cannot approach the presence of God in any way. If God tolerated this behavior, we would constantly see men attempting to steal God's glory so that they can build their own kingdoms. Nowadays, we can approach God; we no longer need a high priest to enter into and make sacrifices on our behalves, since Jesus is our High Priest. Howbeit, the presence of God is still sacred. 1 Samuel 6:19 tells another story about mere men treating the glory, presence and ark of God in a profane way. It reads, "And he smote the men of Bethshemesh, because they had looked into the ark of the LORD, even he smote of the people fifty thousand and threescore and ten men: and the people lamented, because the LORD had smitten many of the people with a great slaughter." If we want to understand the symbolism behind this, consider the moment God placed the cherubim to guard the way of the Tree of Life. These angels had flaming swords. Touching or looking into the ark can be compared to trying to get past those cherubim.

Let's look at four seemingly unrelated scriptures to see if we can connect the dots!

2 Kings 9:1-3	Luke 8:43-46	John 20:15-17	John 20:26-29
And Elisha the prophet called one of the children of the prophets, and said unto him, Gird up thy loins, and take this	And a woman having an issue of blood twelve years, which had spent all her living upon physicians, neither could be	Jesus saith unto her, Woman, why weepest thou? Whom seekest thou? She, supposing him to be the gardener, saith unto	And after eight days again his disciples were within, and Thomas with them: then came Jesus, the doors being shut, and

2 Kings 9:1-3	Luke 8:43-46	John 20:15-17	John 20:26-29
box of oil in thine hand, and go to Ramothgilead: And when thou comest thither, look out there Jehu the son of Jehoshaphat the son of Nimshi, and go in, and make him arise up from among his brethren, and carry him to an inner chamber; then take the box of oil, and pour it on his head, and say, Thus saith the LORD, I have anointed thee king over Israel. Then open the door, and flee, and tarry not.	healed of any, Came behind him, and touched the border of his garment: and immediately her issue of blood stanched. And Jesus said, Who touched me? When all denied, Peter and they that were with him said, Master, the multitude throng thee and press thee, and sayest thou, Who touched me? And Jesus said, Somebody hath touched me: for I perceive that virtue is gone out of me.	him, Sir, if thou have borne him hence, tell me where thou hast laid him, and I will take him away. Jesus saith unto her, Mary. She turned herself, and saith unto him, Rabboni; which is to say, Master. Jesus saith unto her, Touch me not; for I am not yet ascended to my Father: but go to my brethren, and say unto them, I ascend unto my Father, and your Father; and to my God, and your God.	stood in the midst, and said, Peace be unto you. Then saith he to Thomas, Reach hither thy finger, and behold my hands; and reach hither thy hand, and thrust it into my side: and be not faithless, but believing. And Thomas answered and said unto him, My Lord and my God. Jesus saith unto him, Thomas, because thou hast seen me, thou hast believed: blessed are they that have not seen, and yet have believed.

Let's start with 2 Kings 9. The anointing oil that a prophet carried was considered holy. It meant that not one drop of that oil was supposed to touch the prophet (and vice versa). Consider what would have happened had the prophet touched Jehu after the oil had been poured. The prophet's fingerprints would have been on the newly anointed king, and remember, the fingerprints of a man are symbolic of his character. In other words, God didn't want the prophet to make an impression on Jehu. This was a sacred moment! God wanted Jehu's mind on Him and the assignment He'd just given him, not the prophet! The prophet's assignment wasn't to stick around and be praised; his job was to fulfill the assignment God had given him and then make an impromptu exit. In other words, God wanted this particular prophet to be a breath, not a wind or a personality.

Consider the prophet in 1 Kings 13. Let's look at the story.

1 Kings 13:1-5

And, behold, there came a man of God out of Judah by the word of the LORD unto Bethel: and Jeroboam stood by the altar to burn incense. And he cried against the altar in the word of the LORD, and said, O altar, altar, thus saith the LORD; Behold, a child shall be born unto the house of David, Josiah by name; and upon thee shall he offer the priests of the high places that burn incense upon thee, and men's bones shall be burnt upon thee. And he gave a sign the same day, saying, This is the sign which the LORD hath spoken; Behold, the altar shall be rent, and the ashes that are upon it shall be poured out. And it came to pass, when king Jeroboam heard the saying of the man of God, which had cried against the altar in Bethel, that he put forth his hand from the altar, saying, Lay hold on him. And his hand, which he put forth against him, dried up, so that he could not pull it in again to him. **The altar also was rent**, and the ashes poured out from the altar, according to the sign which the man of God had given by the word of the LORD.

1 Kings 13:11-18

Now there dwelt an old prophet in Bethel; and his sons came and told him all the works that the man of God had done that day in Bethel: the words which he had spoken unto the king, them they told also to their father. And their father said unto them, What way went he? For his sons had seen what way the man of God went, which came from Judah. And he said unto his sons, Saddle me the ass. So they saddled him the ass: and he rode thereon, and went after the man of God, and found him sitting under an oak: and he said unto him, Art thou the man of God that camest from Judah? And he said, I am. Then he said unto him, Come home with me, and eat bread. And he said, I may not return with thee, nor go in with thee: neither will I eat bread nor drink water with thee in this place: **For it was said to me by the word of the LORD, Thou shalt eat no bread nor drink water there, nor turn again to go by the way that thou camest**. He said unto him, I am a prophet also as thou art; and an angel spake unto me by the word of the LORD, saying, Bring him back with thee into thine house, that he may eat bread and drink water. But he lied unto him.

1 Kings 13:20-25

And it came to pass, as they sat at the table, that the word of the LORD came unto the prophet that brought him back: And he cried unto the man of God that came from Judah, saying, Thus saith the LORD, Forasmuch as thou hast disobeyed the mouth of the LORD, and hast not kept the commandment which the LORD thy God commanded thee, but camest back, and hast eaten bread and drunk water in the place, of the which the LORD did say to thee, Eat no bread, and drink no water; thy carcase shall not come unto the sepulchre of thy fathers. And it came to pass, after he had eaten bread, and after he had drunk, that he saddled for him the ass, to wit, for the prophet whom he had brought back. And when he was gone, a lion met him by the way, and slew him: and his carcase was cast in the way, and the ass stood by it, the lion also stood by the carcase. And, behold, men passed by, and saw the carcase cast in the way, and the lion standing by the carcase: and they came and told it in the city where the old prophet dwelt.

Again, the prophet's assignment wasn't to stick around and be praised! He was to simply follow whatever instructions God had given him, and then, get out of town as fast as he could. Why is this? God wanted the people to focus on the message, not the messenger! This prophet's job was to be a breath of God in a place that had rejected Him. Through the prophet, God blew His breath against the altar, and the altar split. That was it; the prophet's job was done! Now, all he had to do was get out of that wicked place. But because of what took place between the prophet and the king (a man of great influence), the word spread quickly. Before long, it had reached the old prophet who, in turn, wanted to have lunch with the man who everyone was talking about, and he was willing to lie to make this happen. This is exactly what God had been trying to avoid! He wanted them to focus on His words, not the mouthpiece! Remember, this is reminiscent of what took place with one-third of God's angels! Lucifer's body was made of instruments and precious jewels. He was beautiful to behold! His job was to go into the presence of God, absorb His light and express it before the angels! All the same, whenever the angels worshiped God, the sound of their worship would pass through Lucifer's body and fill the heavens! When God spoke to His angels, His voice would past through Lucifer's body as well. So, the angels would see the glory of God radiating and illuminating through Lucifer, and they'd hear the beautiful sound of God piercing the atmosphere. They would then bow down and worship Him. In other words, Lucifer was a mediator! But one of the dangers of being a mediator is that it is easy to steal God's glory and eventually develop an appetite for it. When the prophet sat down to eat with the older prophet, his appearance in Bethel suddenly became less about God and more about himself. In other words, unbeknownst to him, he'd just robbed God of what belongs to Him—His glory! This means that he'd touched something that was sacred!

As for the woman with the issue of blood, the moment she crawled through the crowd to touch the hem of Jesus' garment was a symbolic one. Think back to the story of Esther. When Esther was charged by Mordecai to go before the king, she said, "All the king's servants and the people of the king's provinces know that if any man or woman goes to the king inside the inner court without being called, there is but one law—to be put to death, except the one to whom the king holds out the golden scepter so that he may live. But as for me, I have not been called to come in to the king these thirty days." This was symbolic of the Old Testament. Only the High Priests could go into the Inner Room of the Tabernacle. Howbeit, when the woman with the issue of blood crawled through the crowd, she violated many traditions and rules! She approached God on her own behalf! So, this act was symbolic of the New Covenant. She came up from behind the Lord. To understand this, let's revisit a chart.

Front of God	Back of God
Alpha	Omega
Beginning	End
Genesis	Revelation
Abba (Father)	Jesus (Son)

Do you see the symbolism here?! She approached revelation; she approached the End of Old Covenant and the Beginning of the New Covenant. She approached the Son to access the Father! Let's look a little deeper! Let's go back to the book of Genesis! Consider what happened after YAHWEH expelled both Adam and Eve from the Garden of Eden. Genesis 3:22-24 reads, "And the LORD God said, Behold, the man is become as one of us, to know good and evil: and now, lest he put forth his hand, and take also of the **tree of life**, and eat, and live for ever: Therefore the LORD God sent him forth from the garden of Eden, to till the ground from whence he was taken. So he drove out the man; and he placed at the east of the garden of Eden Cherubims, and a flaming sword which turned every way, to keep the way of the tree of life. So he drove out the man; and he placed at the east of the garden of Eden Cherubims, and a flaming sword which turned every way, to keep the way of the tree of life." Do you see that?! God said to Himself, "Look, man has become like us! He now knows good and evil, so if we don't remove him from the Garden of Eden, he will eat from the Tree of Life and live forever!" Hear me—Jesus is the Tree of Life! In John 6:54-58, He went on record saying, "Whoso eateth my flesh, and drinketh my blood, hath eternal life; and I will raise him up at the last day. For my flesh is meat indeed, and my blood is drink indeed. He that eateth my flesh, and drinketh my blood, dwelleth in me, and I in him. As the living **Father hath sent me**, and I live by the Father: so he that eateth me, even he shall live by me. This is that bread which **came down from heaven**: not as your fathers did eat manna, and are dead: he that eateth of this bread shall live for ever." While the Cherubim guarded the way to the Tree of Life, God uprooted that Tree from Heaven and sent Him down to Earth so that we could partake of Him! So, when the woman with the issue of blood approached Jesus, she wasn't just touching the hem of His garment, she was pulling back the veil that separated man from God! And what did we have? An issue of blood, of course! She touched the New Covenant!

In John 20, we witness Mary Magdalene having an encounter with Jesus near the tomb where they'd buried His body. Jesus appeared to Mary, and at first, she didn't recognize Him. Eventually, her eyes and understanding were opened, and she realize that the man in front of her was none other than Jesus Christ! Before she could touch Him, Jesus responded, "Touch me not; for I am not yet ascended to my Father." Other translations render Jesus' words this way, "Do not cling to me!" Again, this is prophetic symbolism! Theologians have long debated on the reasoning behind this odd request, but if you look at biblical patterns, you'll be able to see a trend! Mary Magdalene referred to Jesus as "Teacher" and "Rabboni" which, of course, meant that her view of Him was severely limited to the Old Testament. In other words, she couldn't yet grab hold of the Tree of Life because, while she was a loyal follower of Jesus, she hadn't yet grasped the fact that He was and is the Son of God! Had she touched Him, she would have died! But, what about the Apostle Thomas? After all, he'd doubted that the man who'd appeared to the other apostles earlier was Jesus. First and foremost, the fact that the apostles were all together, but he was out somewhere doing his own thing spoke volumes within itself! Next, he didn't trust them enough to believe their words, even though they were all saying the same thing. And finally, he became a contrary wind when he said, "Except I shall see in his hands the print of the nails, and put my finger into the print of the nails, and thrust my hand into his side, I will not believe." Hear me—Thomas was a typecast of Judas Iscariot, and Judas Iscariot had been a typecast of Lucifer!

Again, what did God mean when He said, "Touch not my anointed?" Was He warning us to not utter evil words or physically harm other believers? Yes, that's part of it, but for the most part, He was telling us to place emphasis on His presence, whether He presented Himself to us through a prophet, a widow or any other medium. In short, He was warning us to keep what is sacred … sacred! If we can do this on a personal level, it'll be easy to do this on a corporate level. The more we revere what is sacred to God, the more influence He can trust us with because He'll know that we won't follow in Lucifer's footsteps. This is why the Bible tells us that the first level of ministry is self-control (discipline) and self-deliverance (removing the speck from our own eyes). When we are able to manage our own breaths, God can trust us to become winds of influence, first reaching our families and eventually covering more ground. Look at the chart below. It was taken from the Storm Prediction Center, but it details the strength of wind (force), the speed of wind (knots) and how the World Meteorological Organization classifies each measure of wind. You'll also see how the wind behaves on water, as well as on land. Compare this information to influence.

			Appearance of Wind Effects	
Force	Wind (Knots)	WMO Classification	On the Water	On the Land
0	Less than 1	Calm	Sea surface smooth and mirror-like	Calm, smoke rises vertically
1	1-3	Light Air	Scaly ripples, no foam crests	Smoke drift indicates wind direction, still wind vanes
2	4-6	Light Breeze	Small wavelets, crests glassy, no breaking	Wind felt on face, leaves rustle, vanes begin to move
3	7-10	Gentle Breeze	Large wavelets, crests begin to break, scattered whitecaps	Leaves and small twigs constantly moving, light flags extended
4	11-16	Moderate Breeze	Small waves 1-4 ft. becoming longer, numerous whitecaps	Dust, leaves, and loose paper lifted, small tree branches move
5	17-21	Fresh Breeze	Moderate waves 4-8 ft taking longer form, many whitecaps, some spray	Small trees in leaf begin to sway
6	22-27	Strong Breeze	Larger waves 8-13 ft, whitecaps common, more spray	Larger tree branches moving, whistling in wires
7	28-33	Near Gale	Sea heaps up, waves 13-19 ft, white foam streaks off breakers	Whole trees moving, resistance felt walking against wind
8	34-40	Gale	Moderately high (18-25 ft) waves of greater length, edges of crests begin to break into spindrift, foam blown in streaks	Twigs breaking off trees, generally impedes progress
9	41-47	Strong Gale	High waves (23-32 ft), sea begins to roll, dense streaks of foam, spray may reduce visibility	Slight structural damage occurs, slate blows off roofs
10	48-55	Storm	Very high waves (29-41 ft) with overhanging crests, sea white with densely blown foam,	Seldom experienced on land, trees broken or uprooted, "considerable structural damage"

			Appearance of Wind Effects	
11	56-63	Violent Storm	heavy rolling, lowered visibility Exceptionally high (37-52 ft) waves, foam patches cover sea, visibility more reduced	
12	64	Hurricane	Air filled with foam, waves over 45 ft, sea completely white with driving spray, visibility greatly reduced	

Source: Storm Prediction Center/Beaufort Wind Scale/Developed in 1805 by Sir Francis Beaufort, U.K. Royal Navy/

I shared this chart to demonstrate the power of influence. The amount of force behind each person or wind would determine what amount of distance that individual travels and how much impact he or she has. Your measure of influence is, of course, measured by the number of people you influence, but your impact is measured by the way in which you influence these people. If you don't see the presence or the Word of God as holy, you will negatively impact how others see Him as well. You would then repeat Lucifer's sin. When Lucifer deceived one-third of God's angels, he'd done this by using his breath (influence).

Luke 10:18
And he said unto them, I beheld Satan as lightning fall from heaven.

Revelation 12:4
And his tail drew the third part of the stars of heaven, and did cast them to the earth.

Remember, your goal is to influence yourself; this way, you will positively influence and impact the lives of others. It starts with self-control (discipline), and once your voice is able to change you, God will use your voice to reach and change others. But He's not looking to have a do-over of what occurred in Heaven when Lucifer and his angels fell from glory.

MEDITATION MOMENT

The earth is the LORD'S, and the fulness thereof; the world, and they that dwell therein. For he hath founded it upon the seas, and established it upon the floods. Who shall ascend into the hill of the LORD? or who shall stand in his holy place? He that hath clean hands, and a pure heart; who hath not lifted up his soul unto vanity, nor sworn deceitfully. He shall receive the blessing from the LORD, and righteousness from the God of his salvation. This is the generation of them that seek him, that seek thy face, O Jacob. Selah. Lift up your heads, O ye gates; and be ye lift up, ye everlasting doors; and the King of glory shall come in. Who is this King of glory? The LORD strong and mighty, the LORD mighty in battle. Lift up your heads, O ye gates; even lift them up, ye everlasting doors; and the King of glory shall come in. Who is this King of glory? The LORD of hosts, he is the King of glory. Selah.

What are the meditation points for you? List them below.

Meditation Points	
1	
2	
3	
4	
5	
6	
7	
8	
9	
10	
11	
12	
13	
14	
15	

WORD STUDY

List the words that stand out to you and conduct a word study.
Again, if you don't have space in this document, use another document.

Word	

Definition or Etymology

Word	

Definition or Etymology

Word	

Definition or Etymology

LET'S REFLECT!

_____

_____

_____

_____

_____

_____

_____

_____

_____

_____

_____

_____

MY ALARM CLOCK

Did You Know?
Up to 15% of our population are sleepwalkers.

Did You Know?
We forget 50% of our dreams.

Did You Know?
Lack of sleep increases the risk of Alzheimer's.

Did You Know?
The average person takes seven to ten minutes to fall asleep.

Did You Know?
Meditation activate parts of the brain that control sleep.

Using the boxes below, record the dates when you had trouble sleeping.
Did you meditate that night? Write yes or no in the box provided.

Monday	Tuesday	Wednesday	Thursday	Friday	Saturday	Sunday

THE ART OF MEDITATION

Meditation (Etymology)
c. 1200, meditacioun, "contemplation; devout preoccupation; private devotions, prayer," from Old French meditacion "thought, reflection, study," and directly from Latin meditationem (nominative meditatio) "a thinking over, meditation," noun of action from past-participle stem of meditari "to meditate, think over, reflect, consider," from a frequentative form of PIE root *med- "take appropriate measures." Meaning "meditative discourse on a subject" is early 14c.; meaning "act of meditating, continuous calm thought upon some subject" is from late 14c. The Latin verb also had stronger senses: "plan, devise, practice, rehearse, study."
Source: Online Etymology Dictionary

Word	Origin	Meaning
Hagah	Hebrew	to moan, growl, utter, speak, muse
Enthumeomai	Greek	to reflect on, to ponder
Meletaó	Greek	to care for, practice, study
Siach	Hebrew	to muse, complain, talk (of)

Scriptures	
Chapter and Verse	**Text**
Psalm 19:14	Let the words of my mouth and the meditation of my heart be acceptable in your sight, O Lord, my rock and my redeemer.
Psalm 119:15	I will meditate on your precepts and fix my eyes on your ways.
Joshua 1:8	This Book of the Law shall not depart from your mouth, but you shall meditate on it day and night, so that you may be careful to do according to all that is written in it. For then you will make your way prosperous, and then you will have good success.
Isaiah 26:3	You will keep in perfect peace those whose minds are steadfast, because they trust in you.
Philippians 4:8	Finally, brothers and sisters, whatever is true, whatever is noble, whatever is right, whatever is pure, whatever is lovely, whatever is admirable—if anything is excellent or praiseworthy—think about such things.

| Psalm 104:34 | Let my meditation be pleasing to Him; as for me, I shall be glad in the Lord. |

In short, the word "meditate" means to contemplate, to think and to ponder. It means to bring something to the forefront of your mind again and again with the sole purpose of committing something to memory. It means to preoccupy your mind with a certain word, picture or thought. Remember, there are three dimensions or levels of the mind. Note: the chart below was taken from Stone Psychology.

Conscious	Subconscious	Unconscious
5-10% of your mind	Approximately 80-90% of the mind	Approximately 5-10% of the mind
Thinking	Semi-automatic Psychological Systems	Automatic Psychological Systems
Rational	Holds Beliefs About the World	Early Impressions (In Utero, Birth, First Year)
Logical	Holds Beliefs About Self	
Planning	Habits, Thoughts, Emotions	
Sets Goals	Fight or Flight Response	Instinctual Responses
Knows What You Want	Remembered Trauma	Forgotten Trauma
Short Term Memory	Long Term Memory	Cellular Memory
	Protection	
	Fears	
	Desires	

(Source: Stone Psychology/Conscious, Subconscious, Unconscious)

Conscious	Subconscious	Unconscious
30 Fold	60 Fold	100 Fold
Outer Court	**Inner Court**	**Most Holy Place**
Body	**Soul**	**Spirit**

Our conscious deals with the surface of our minds; it is pretty much the outer courts of our thinking. Our subconscious, on the other hand, is the area that has the most traffic (thought-wise). It's where we store the majority of our memories. The subconscious is what the Bible refers to as the heart. The goal of meditation is to take a thought from the outer courts of the mind (conscious) and bring that thought to the inner courts (subconscious) where it becomes an extension of ourselves. Consider Isaiah 14, where God deals with Lucifer about what he had been meditating on. Isaiah 14:12-14 reads, "How art thou fallen from heaven, O Lucifer, son of the morning! how art thou cut down to the ground, which didst weaken the nations! For **thou hast said in thine heart**, I will ascend into heaven, I will exalt my throne above the stars of God: I will sit also upon the mount of the congregation, in the sides of the north: I will ascend above the heights of the clouds; I will be like the most High." Lucifer's crime first took place in his heart. In other words, it wasn't just a thought in passing as we so frequently have. It was a thought that he'd pondered on again and again until it finally found its way into his heart. From there, it started to twist his mind all the more until he was consumed with the imaginations, fantasies and thoughts of being like YAHWEH. And it didn't stop there. He then gathered the angels of God in darkness and began to spew his lies and his evil plans into their hearing. In essence, he became one with the thought, so his spirit took the shape of his heart; this is why he is now Satan, which means adversary.

What Lucifer did was meditate on a thought, and hear me—to meditate doesn't mean that you have to sit down in what is commonly referred to as "Indian style" or what some occultic movements refer to as "Padmasana," which is commonly known as the "Lotus." Most of these positions are less than two hundred years old and are rooted in non-western cultures and extra-biblical beliefs. They aren't necessarily demonic unless, of course, the individual is using them to praise, worship, summon or pay homage to a false deity. Most Christians who, for example, do yoga and practice many of the positions used by Hindus to worship false gods do so without knowing the origin of those postures. Does this mean that they are outside the will of God and headed towards a fiery grave? No, of course not. It's no different than you celebrating Christmas and many holidays that have pagan roots, symbolism and practices—unknowingly! You're only in error if you accept those beliefs as your own. If I decided to create my own form of exercise that incorporated mental, spiritual and physical activities, I would obviously use scriptures and a lot of Christian symbolism to establish my new practice. If it took off and a group of Atheists, Satanists and other non-believers were to start practicing my new form, would they automatically become Christian? Or would it lead them to Christ? No and no! They'd focus on the benefits of my new exercise, all the while, ignoring the man, the mind and the beliefs behind the movement. Of course, this isn't to encourage believers to follow after false religions, embrace their ideologies or ignore the symbolism behind their practices, this is to release you from the fear that commonly surrounds these things.

To meditate means to take a thought that's either in the conscious (above the surface of the mind) or the subconscious (underneath the surface of the mind) and intentionally ponder on that thought. Again, the goal of meditation is to discipline the mind. Hear me—a mind that's undisciplined is one without borders, boundaries, rules or regulations. This means that the person is led by his or her flesh. Another way to say this is, the person is emotional. Emotional people are unstable, untrustworthy and imbalanced. And by imbalanced, I mean they give more weight, priority, or value to their feelings than they do to logic; this is what makes them emotional.

According to Healthline, meditation has 12 benefits.

Reduces Stress	Controls Anxiety	Promotes Emotional Health
Enhances Self-Awareness	Lengthens Attention Span	May Reduce Age-Related Memory Loss
Can Generate Kindness	May Help Fight Addictions	Improves Sleep
Helps Control Pain	Can Decrease Blood Pressure	You Can Meditate Anywhere

Again, meditation isn't a pagan practice. The Bible tells us to meditate on God's Word, His ways (principles), His precepts and all that He has done. After the Exodus from Egypt, Moses told the Israelites, "Remember this day, in which ye came out from Egypt, out of the house of bondage; for by strength of hand the LORD brought you out from this place: there shall no leavened bread be eaten" (Exodus 13:3). Notice that he didn't tell Israel to remember their bondage, but to remember the day that they came out of bondage. Hear me—people who think or center their minds around their traumas often deal with unforgiveness, bitterness, fear and conditions like PTSD (Post Traumatic Stress Syndrome). But people who remember or place emphasis on their deliverance are oftentimes bold and full of faith. The goal of meditation is to increase your faith, not diminish it. If you are meditating on the wrong things, of course, meditation will then have an adverse effect. The goal is to take the Word of God and all that is Godly from the outer courts of your mind and usher it into your Most Holy Place or, at minimum, into your subconscious. This way, you can pull it to your conscious mind as often as possible, and from there, you can drive it deeper and deeper into your subconscious through meditation. This is similar to taking food and chewing it again and again until you can easily swallow it. This allows you to extract more nutrients from the food, and it allows the saliva in your mouth to break down the food for easier digestion.

Imaginations and Preoccupations

2 Corinthians 10:5 reads, "Casting down imaginations, and every high thing that exalteth itself against the knowledge of God, and bringing into captivity every thought to the obedience of Christ." The word "imagination" obviously comes from the word "image." The mind processes thoughts this way—we see images or imagery in our minds; this, of course, is what we refer to as our imagination. Once we see an image, we use several modes of communication to express what we've seen; they are: words, drawings, sign language, body language (this includes facial expressions) and symbols. Of course, this isn't an exhaustive list; this is a list of our most commonly used modes of expression.

Most of our imaginations come from our conscious and subconscious minds. The way that it works is, we hear a song. That song will play in our conscious minds until it is committed or permitted into the subconscious. From there, our minds will continually pull this song up, especially if something or someone brings this song to remembrance. So, in essence, we create a mental playlist in our minds, and there are so many triggers or buttons that will activate those playlists at any given moment. For example, you may be sitting in church when, all of a sudden, a young lady passes you by wearing a long red dress, red heels and red lipstick. If you are a young, single, heterosexual male, you may find yourself humming songs that incorporate the phrase "red dress," for example, you may start immediately thinking about Johnny Gill's classic hit, "My, My, My." It doesn't mean that you're lusting after the woman; you may simply be attracted to her, and because Johnny Gill's song was stored in your memory bank, the sight of the woman only served to trigger that particular song. Now, if you've been watching shows that demean or degrade women, the sight of the woman may trigger a more sinister and perverse thought. The problem isn't that the woman wore a red dress to church, after all, there's absolutely nothing ungodly about colors. The problem is what's in your heart. These are the images that you've subjected your mind to over and over again. This is why the Bible tells us to guard our hearts. Let's look at a few scriptures.

Colossians 3:2	Philippians 4:8	Genesis 5:5	Mark 11:24
Set your minds on things that are above, not on things that are on earth.	Finally, brothers, whatever is true, whatever is honorable, whatever is just, whatever is pure, whatever is lovely, whatever is commendable, if there	And God saw that the wickedness of man was great in the earth, and that every imagination of the thoughts of his heart was only evil continually.	Therefore I tell you, whatever you ask in prayer, believe that you have received it, and it will be yours.

Colossians 3:2	Philippians 4:8	Genesis 5:5	Mark 11:24
	is any excellence, if there is anything worthy of praise, think about these things.		

Set your mind, think about, imagine or believe—all of these have to do with what we subject or immerse our minds in. In other words, we have control over our minds. Sure, you may find your mind being inundated with perverse thoughts, blasphemous words and ungodly rhetoric, but all this means is that, at some point, your mind had been subjected to these things, and somehow, they managed to make their way into your subconscious. It can also mean that you are in need of deliverance. To combat this, God tells us to (intentionally) set our minds on the things that are above, to think about what is pure, and to simply have faith in Him. This is how we manage the real estate that is our minds. And hear me, the mind is broad and wide and deep; it is without ends or limitations. It is a canvas that God wants to paint on, and of course, Satan would love to express himself on it as well. The mind is like the moon. There are many unexplored parts to it; all the same, there are some areas that have been explored, but not necessarily claimed. Then again, we do have those areas that we've gotten full control over. Any area that is unclaimed is an area that is dark; this doesn't mean that it's evil, it means that it is without revelation. And Satan will attempt to occupy any area or zone where he sees darkness (voids, absence of information); this way, he can influence us in those areas. For example, let's talk about your encounter with the woman in the red dress or, if you're a woman, let's deal with your encounter with the man in the red car. Your thoughts in relation to this person should be pure, but if the area connected to your sexuality has not been conquered and submitted to God, you may find yourself having impure thoughts about the person. To conquer or reconquer this area, you would potentially have to go through deliverance and learn healthier ways to view the opposite sex.

It goes without saying, your imagination can be used for good, just as it can be used for evil. God originally designed this function of our minds so that we could:

1. **See the Vision:** create and preview a mental snapshot of our personalized promised lands before we enter them.
2. **Write the Vision:** create the blueprint for whatever it is that we want (or plan) to have or build. For this to be effective, we have to convert the thought from the realm of our imaginations to the natural realm by recording it on paper or using some other form of technology.

3. **Make it Plain:** this is when we spell the vision out into minute details; this is called chewing or breaking down the vision.

4. **Count the Costs:** breaking the vision down allows us to not only price the materials and resources we'll need to bring our imaginations from the spirit realm (thoughts) to the Earth's realm, but it also allows us to preview what we stand to lose and gain if we are to implement our plans. For example, there are people who know they are called to write books, but they know that the minute they publish their first books, they will lose some relationships. In other words, they've counted the cost. And many of them have decided that it's not worth it, while others have decided to assume the risks involved to help others.

5. **Encourage Ourselves in the Lord:** After counting the costs and starting the building process, the imagination allows us to encourage ourselves whenever we start dealing with the warfare associated with building. This function allows us to remember what God has brought us out of, what we've accomplished thus far, and it allows us to look into the lives of other believers to see what they've endured while building.

The mind is a wonderful instrument when it's in the hands of the Lord. Again, it has no ends; in other words, you are not limited to what you can accomplish. God didn't place a cap on your earning or your learning. Every cap or limitation placed on the human mind was placed there by the human himself or herself. Consider the slaves brought to America starting in 1619. It was illegal for them to learn to read and write. All the same, it was illegal for Whites to teach Blacks how to read or write. But while this made it difficult for African Americans to be educated, it didn't necessarily prevent them from getting an education. There were some men and women who secretly learned to read and write. What this means is that every cap that is placed on the human mind can be removed by the person wearing it; that is, if the individual is willing to assume the risks involved. So, if you decided today that you want to earn $45 billion, there is nothing that can stop you from reaching your goal but yourself. Sure, Satan and mankind could make it difficult, but if you're willing to deal with the frustrations, the betrayals, the setbacks, the setups, the losses, and the breakdowns, you will eventually reach your goal. In short, what you have to do is take control of your imaginations and set your mind on Godly things. Consider your car's GPS. Whatever you set it to will determine where you go; that is, if you follow instructions, of course. This is what it means to set your mind. Consider Ecclesiastes 1:13, which reads, "And I gave my heart to seek and search out by wisdom concerning all things that are done under heaven: this sore travail hath God given to the sons of man to be exercised therewith." First and foremost, the author of this text (King Solomon) was having a moment of deep thought where he had been meditating on the concept of vanity and the elusiveness of material wealth. If you'll follow the entire book of Ecclesiastes, you'll notice that all the way up until the eight chapter, King Solomon was preoccupied with thoughts and talks of how valueless and meaningless material wealth is. He pondered on the value of wisdom and compared it to the foolishness of gain. Remember, King Solomon was the richest king to ever live. And it was through his gain of material wealth that he concluded that it was all pointless, useless, and vain, especially considering how short our time on Earth is. These preoccupations didn't keep him from falling into the beds of pagan women, however; they just made him more aware of his mortality. In other words, you can meditate on death, the futility of material wealth and all that is vain, but if you don't set your mind to the things of God, it's only a matter of time before whatever it is you've been preoccupying your mind with materializes.

To get control of your imagination, you have to replace every negative and perverse thought with something good. Hear me—this is no easy task! You'll have to be consistent and unrelenting for this to work, otherwise, whatever you've been subjected to will keep surfacing until you resolve within your heart that you can't defeat the thoughts. For example, if you keep having sexually perverse thoughts, you'd overcome them by:

1. **Casting the imaginations down:** this doesn't mean that you audibly say to the imaginations, "I cast you down!" It simply means that you place another thought above or higher than that particular thought. For example, let's go back to the woman in the red dress. If your thoughts about her are impure, you'd simply imagine her the way God designed her, but before you can do this, you have to call the impure imaginations what they are—perverse! This causes the mind to file the imagination in the dump files associated with your conscious mind.

2. **See her the way that God sees her:** You'd imagine her fully clothed, preaching or teaching the Word and casting out devils. If she oozed seduction every time she passed you by, you'd have to overcome her present state by imagining who God has called and designed her to be.

3. **Intercede on her behalf:** You'd pray for her deliverance, but not before praying for your own. Remember, don't address the speck in someone else's eye when you have one in your own.

The goal here is for you to retake or reconquer your mind! Another way to do this is through:

1. **Reading the Bible:** How can you know or ponder on God's will if you don't know His Word?

2. **Reading books:** There are many books on the markets that target the areas of your mind that you want to weaken and the areas of your mind that you want to strengthen.

3. **Going to therapy:** Therapy helps to address the human side of your struggles. Therapists focus on the past to help you better understand why you are in the condition that you're in; this is so you'll have a brighter, healthier future.

4. **Going through deliverance:** This deals with the spiritual side of your struggles.

5. **Changing your environment:** In order for a change to take place internally, one must be initiated and followed through externally. This includes changing what you listen to, who you listen to, who you surround yourself with and what you immerse yourself in.

After this, you have to preoccupy your mind with good and Godly thoughts. Again, this is a wrestling match, so you have to be persistent and consistent. For example, imagine yourself at peace. What thoughts pop up when you imagine this? Do you imagine yourself in a house surrounded by water or do you imagine yourself being at a spa? Whatever thoughts follow the concept of peace are directly connected to a memory or an image. Maybe you saw a video commercial about a house nestled in the middle of an island, surrounded by water, or maybe it was an imagination created out of necessity. Either way, the word "peace" triggered a response from your subconscious. Again, this is the seat of your belief system. But if the thought of peace made you think about divorcing your spouse, disconnecting from your family or cutting off all of your friends, this would mean that you've attached the word "chaos" to your relationships. This doesn't mean that it's true, after all, you could potentially be the toxic person in those relationships, but either way, you have decided (decision is the settling of the mind on a belief) that peace can be found outside of your most intimate relationships. To remedy this, you'd need to follow the five steps above and meditate on what's good in all of your relationships. You and the people connected to you may also need therapy. Understand this—relational therapy is not necessarily centered around fixing the people in your life, it's more directed at:

1. Helping everyone to realize and confront their individual issues.
2. Helping everyone to pull down unrealistic expectations.
3. Helping the parties involved to confront unaddressed problems in the relationship.
4. Helping you all to create a healthy connection.
5. Giving you all the tools needed to address and confront future issues that may arise.

Please note that in order for therapy to work, everyone involved must have an open mind, a willingness to learn and the ability to receive correction. When people go into therapy expecting the therapist to side with them and echo their concerns or sentiments to their loved ones, they often leave their sessions disappointed, with no plans whatsoever to return.

In summary, you have to allow the Word of God to occupy every corner of your thinking, and you have to preoccupy every space that has not been fully changed by Him with good and Godly thoughts. The areas that have not been changed are the areas where you'll find your voids, and these voids are the direct results of trauma, a lack of information and the presence of misinformation. You preoccupy these areas by focusing on something good and repeatedly centering your mind around that thought. And of course, you need to invite the Holy Spirit into those areas so that He can fill them, heal them and give you the revelation you'll need to produce fruits in those areas.

The Fruits of the Holy Spirit

In order for a plant to grow, it needs the following:

Covering	Nutrients	Water
Sunlight	Oxygen	Carbon Dioxide
Space and Time	The Right Temperature	Garden

Covering

The normal covering for a plant is soil, but a plant doesn't absolutely have to have soil to grow. What soil provides is a covering; this keeps the plant from being overexposed to sunlight. It also protects the plants roots from certain pests, and it provides the plants with nutrients. Soil or the covering represents the body or, better yet, the flesh of a man.

Nutrients

This, of course, represents the Word of God. Jesus said it this way, "But he answered and said, It is written, Man shall not live by bread alone, but by every word that proceedeth out of the mouth of God."

Water

Water symbolizes many things including purification, salvation and the Holy Spirit.

Sunlight

Light is used to represent revelation. Without revelation, man walks in darkness and cannot grow.

Oxygen

This represents the air we breathe or, better yet, the Spirit of God. He is the Giver of life; without Him, we would be spiritually dead.

Carbon Dioxide

Carbon dioxide is necessary for plant health, life and development. During the photosynthesis process, carbon dioxide pairs up with water and sunlight to produce sugar molecules and oxygen. In other words, it uses the resources provided to the plant and aids in creating plant food (carbohydrates) for the plant. This, of course, represents your pastor. Having a pastor not only keeps us accountable, but this keeps us from becoming subject to our own interpretations of the Bible, and from being blown away by the many winds of false doctrine.

Space and Time

This represents the room needed for an individual to grow, make mistakes, learn from those mistakes and eventually mature. If you smother a gift with attention, compliments, complaints or expectations, that gift won't have what he or she needs to grow beyond the issues that he or she wrestles with.

The Right Temperature

This represents our attitude. The wrong attitude produces the wrong fruits.

Garden

This, of course, represents community. And while plants can and do grow outside of gardens, the ones that do are often labeled as wildflowers or weeds. Plants located in a garden are intentionally and strategically grown and pruned so that they can repeatedly produce fruit. Wildflowers, on the other hand, often fall subject to predators, disease and harsh weather conditions.

Of course, you are that plant, but within you is a garden. This is where you will grow, are growing or have grown the fruits of the Holy Spirit. But before we delve into this, let's establish one thing—your mind is your mental real estate. It is vast and broad; it is deep and without limitations. What you allow to live in your head will directly impact your life and your lifestyle. This is why you have to cast down evil imaginations and every high thing that exalts itself against the knowledge of God, and after doing this, you have to bring every thought captive to the obedience of Christ. What does this mean? It's simple. You intentionally and consistently inundate your mind with good thoughts, and every time your mind deviates and starts pondering on other things, your goal is to bring it back to the good thoughts. This is the process of pruning. You will have to do this several times, but eventually, your mind will be healthy enough to produce everything your heart desires.

Your imagination is nothing but a preview of what could potentially materialize itself in your life. If the imagination is dark and evil, cast it down by replacing it with a good thought. If the imagination is good, you can still replace it with a better thought. The goal is to strengthen your mind. This is what it means to till the ground of the flesh in order to bring forward spiritual fruits.

Fruits of the Holy Spirit		
Love	Joy	Peace
Forbearance	Kindness	Goodness
Faithfulness	Gentleness	Self Control

Please note that like natural fruits, when these fruits are present, they repeatedly drop seeds, meaning, they slowly begin to cover every area of your mind. Imagine this to be your personal Garden of Eden, and these are the trees that God wants you to plant, water and eat from. You have to grow them all by studying and applying the Word of God to your life. And you'd want to grow them in every area of your life until your mind and your thoughts are filled with what is good and Godly. All the same, you have to free some ground up by uprooting negative, ungodly and toxic thoughts and patterns, and replacing them with positive, Godly and healthy thoughts and patterns. You would have to use the function of your imaginations to constantly inundate your mind with scriptures, good thoughts and all that is God. You have to:

1. **Uproot the weeds:** Have you ever heard someone say, "I'm glad that it wasn't me because I would have cussed everybody out!" What that person is admitting to is having a shortage of self-control and an abundance of pride. What this means is that the area of that person's mind that deals with self-control is full of weeds. Pride is a weed. Anger is a weed. Vengeance, when in the heart of man, is a weed. And these issues can't grow alongside any of the fruits of the Holy Spirit. One will always cancel out the other, and it's typically the one you water and/or source from the most. To grow the fruits of the Holy Spirit, you have to uproot the works of the flesh.

2. **Dress the garden:** The word "dress" in this sense means "to put in order." This means that you have to be strategic and intentional with growing the fruits of the Holy Spirit, prioritizing them over your feelings, fears and preferences.

3. **Water the garden:** Water represents purification. Here's the thing—the flesh comes from the ground; it is represented by dirt. So, while you may, for example, be growing the fruit of kindness, it can and will get some dirt on it. Meaning, it'll be seasoned by your experiences and issues. Remember, out of the heart pours the issues of life. Where do they pour? On your fruits and on the lives of everyone around you. Watering the garden means studying the Word so that you can grow the fruits. It also means removing your personal interpretations, agenda of and opinions from the fruits.

4. **Till the ground of the garden:** The ground is your flesh. You have to constantly uproot the works of the flesh, pull down imaginations, resist all ungodly temptations, deny yourself and take up your cross every single day. The flesh and the Spirit are contrary to one another. You will feed one and starve the other. If you feed your flesh, it will dominate your spirit; if you feed your spirit, you will be led by the Holy Spirit which, of

course, would bring your flesh into submission. Again, this is a daily process!

5. **Monitor the garden:** When Adam and Eve were given charge of the Garden of Eden, they failed to monitor its borders, and we know how that ended. Satan slithered into the Garden and tempted Eve. Hear me—you have to monitor your thoughts! Through this, you'll know when you're in need of deliverance, therapy or when you need to fast, pray or rest! People who don't monitor their gardens often suffer from burnout and depression! Pay attention to your thoughts, especially those thoughts that are prevalent and invasive.

6. **Prune the garden:** This represents the cutting away or restructuring of relationships. There are some people who were great friends of yours when you were in high school, but they may be enemies of your future. This is largely because they are not interested in who you're becoming; they are interested in the character you became when you didn't know who you are! And this isn't limited to relationships from high school. A person's time in your life can literally expire in a matter of weeks or months if the person starts becoming toxic to what God is doing in your life. And just like He expelled Adam and Eve from the Garden of Eden, there are some people you may have to expel from your life or, at minimum, from your inner circle. Pruning the garden means remaining prayerful, watchful and obedient.

7. **Reap what you've sown:** When a harvest is complete, the fruits can be harvested. When reaping this harvest, we are oftentimes humbled because we find other issues that we failed to address—many of which caused delays and a host of issues. At the same time, seeing the fruits of love, joy, peace, forbearance, kindness, goodness, faithfulness, gentleness and self-control helps us to grow (mature) as believers. So, if someone wants to celebrate you, show up! If God wants to highlight something you've done or set a place for you in the presence of your enemies, show up! When the season of harvest comes, our job is to simply show up!

8. **Repeat:** As long as there is breath in your body, you will be dressing and addressing the garden that is your life. Just remember to follow the aforementioned steps and don't try to skip any!

Let's look at the weeds that typically grow in our gardens.

Adultery	Fornication	Uncleanness
Idolatry	Witchcraft	Hatred
Emulations	Wrath	Strife
Heresies	Envyings	Murders

Lasciviousness	Variance	Seditions
Drunkenness		Revelings

All of these are like molds; they grow best in dark environments. All the same, they work against the fruits of the Holy Spirit, so you have to be active and intentional in regards to uprooting them and creating an environment where they cannot grow or thrive. This involves having a steady prayer life, fasting, frequent Bible study, accountability, therapy (if and when needed), deliverance and most of all, a desire to be better.

The Art of Rumination

Meditation is the act of taking an idea, an image or a concept from the conscious to the subconscious, and then regurgitating it from the subconscious to ponder on it some more. It is an intentional process of committing something to memory and extracting all of the wisdom and revelation from the thought by constantly chewing, swallowing and regurgitating it. This is called rumination.

Merriam Webster defines the word "ruminate" this way:
1. to go over in the mind repeatedly and often casually or slowly
2. to chew repeatedly for an extended period
3. to chew again what has been chewed slightly and swallowed: chew the cud
4. to engage in contemplation: reflect

Ruminate (Etymology)

1530s, "to turn over in the mind," also "to chew cud" (1540s), from Latin ruminatus, past participle of ruminare "to chew the cud; turn over in the mind," from rumen (genitive ruminis) "gullet," of uncertain origin. Related: Ruminated; ruminating.

Source: Online Etymology Dictionary

Think about food. In order to break it down, we have to chew it. The benefits of chewing are:
1. It aids in the digestion of the food.
2. Chewing prevents choking on the food.
3. Chewing has been found to make food taste better.
4. Chewing helps you to get full faster. Consequently, you eat less. This helps you maintain a healthy weight.
5. The more you chew, the more nutrients you'll extract from the food.
6. Chewing is good for your teeth because it causes our bodies to produce saliva. Saliva

not only helps to wash away the food debris of what we've eaten, it also aids in the removal and control of bacteria.

How many times should you chew what you eat before attempting to consume it? It depends on what you're eating, but the standard is, at minimum, 32 times. Consider this—the Word of God is oftentimes compared with food in the Bible.

Water	Jesus answered and said unto her, Whosoever drinketh of this water shall thirst again: But whosoever drinketh of the water that I shall give him shall never thirst; but the water that I shall give him shall be in him a well of water springing up into everlasting life. *John 4:13-14*
Milk	As newborn babes, desire the sincere milk of the word, that ye may grow thereby: If so be ye have tasted that the Lord is gracious. *1 Peter 2:2-3*
Bread	Then Jesus said unto them, Verily, verily, I say unto you, Moses gave you not that bread from heaven; but my Father giveth you the true bread from heaven. *John 6:32*
Meat	I have fed you with milk, and not with meat: for hitherto ye were not able to bear it, neither yet now are ye able. *1 Corinthians 3:2*
Honey	How sweet are thy words unto my taste! Yea, sweeter than honey to my mouth! *Psalm 119:103*

The point is, you chew or ruminate on the Word of God just as you'd chew your food. How do you do this? By simply breaking the scriptures down into sections and rehearsing them in your mind. For example, let's take one of my favorite scriptures, which is Psalm 23:1. It reads, "The LORD is my shepherd; I shall not want." To meditate on this scripture, you'd break it down into meditation moments. For example:

First Moment	The Lord
Second Moment	The Lord is my
Third Moment	The Lord is my Shepherd

79

Fourth Moment	I shall not want

This would be the model that you use with any and every scripture. Consider John 3:16, which reads, "For God so loved the world, that he gave his only begotten Son, that whosoever believeth in him should not perish, but have everlasting life."

First Moment	For God so loved
Second Moment	For God so loved the world
Third Moment	That He gave
Fourth Moment	That He gave His only begotten Son

In this, you can start off with, "For God," as well, and you can focus on God all by Himself. He is God, the Almighty; He is Elohim. Do you see how this works? What you're doing is rehearsing the scriptures in your mind and breaking down every individual word so that your mind can digest it. Again, remember the layout of mankind.

Conscious	Subconscious	Unconscious
Egypt	Wilderness	Promised Land

The goal is to take a scripture, a memory or a thought from the wilderness to the Promised Land, but to do this, it has to make its way through your conscious and circle the mountains of the subconscious time and time again until it becomes one with your spirit. In other words, until it reaches the Promised Land. But, in order to do this, you have to ruminate or chew on the Word of God until it gives up its most valuable nutrients: understanding and wisdom.

Toxic Meditation

There are four forms of toxic meditation. They are:

1. **Worry:** this is taking a negative thought and ruminating on it time and time again until it produces fear, anxiety and, of course, doubt. Worry is thinking about the present or the past, and fearing how they will impact the future. This is why Matthew 6:34 tells us, "Take therefore no thought for the morrow: for the morrow shall take thought for the things of itself. Sufficient unto the day *is* the evil thereof."

2. **Anxiousness:** Another word for "anxious" is "impatience." Philippians 4:6 warns us this way, "Be anxious for nothing, but in everything by prayer and supplication, with thanksgiving, let your requests be made known to God." Remember, patience is one of the fruits of the Holy Spirit, and of course, anxiousness produces anxiety as well.

3. **Obsession:** Obsession occurs when a person has no restraint on his or her imagination. When rejection, fantasy, pride, and entitlement link up, they produce the breeding grounds for obsession. What happens is the individual having obsessive thoughts will ruminate on a fantasy because this allows the individual to escape his or her own reality. Some imaginations even cause the release of oxytocin, also known as the "love hormone." Before long, the obsessed individual will become addicted to the fantasies, and eventually, will obsessively try to bring those fantasies to pass. Again, this is a form of meditation.

4. **Unforgiveness:** This means to meditate or reflect on something someone did or said to you over and over again.

In short, toxic meditation is processing and reprocessing information that produces fear, anxiety and a host of negative emotions. The art of meditation was never designed to be used as a tool of torment! For example, if we get a bill in the mail that we can't afford to pay, the majority of us will fixate on that bill until anxiety sets in. This is centered around what we believe will or could potentially happen if the bill is not paid on time. This only serves to make us increasingly anxious, and anxiety negatively impacts both our mental and physical health. For example, anxiety has been known to cause:

1. Heart Problems
2. Breathing Problems
3. Stomach and Gastrointestinal Problems
4. High Blood Pressure
5. Insomnia
6. Weakened Immune System
7. Muscle Tension
8. Fatigue
9. Tremors
10. Excessive Sweating

Of course, these are just a few of the problems often produced by anxiety. And of course, our Bible is riddled with people who've experienced anxiety as the result of meditating on the wrong things. Look at the chart below.

Name	Scripture	
David	Psalm 6:3-4	My soul is also sore vexed: but thou, O LORD, how long? Return, O LORD, deliver my soul: oh save me for thy mercies' sake.
Job	Job 8:6-10	Oh that I might have my request; and that God would grant me the

Name	Scripture	
		thing that I long for! Even that it would please God to destroy me; that he would let loose his hand, and cut me off! Then should I yet have comfort; yea, I would harden myself in sorrow: let him not spare; for I have not concealed the words of the Holy One.
Elijah	1 Kings 19:4	But he himself went a day's journey into the wilderness, and came and sat down under a juniper tree: and he requested for himself that he might die; and said, It is enough; now, O LORD, take away my life; for I am not better than my fathers.
Jeremiah	Jeremiah 20:14-18	Cursed be the day wherein I was born: let not the day wherein my mother bare me be blessed. Cursed be the man who brought tidings to my father, saying, A man child is born unto thee; making him very glad. And let that man be as the cities which the LORD overthrew, and repented not: and let him hear the cry in the morning, and the shouting at noontide; because he slew me not from the womb; or that my mother might have been my grave, and her womb to be always great with me. Wherefore came I forth out of the womb to see labor and sorrow, that my days should be consumed with shame?
Jesus	John 12:27-28	Now is my soul troubled; and what shall I say? Father, save me from this hour: but for this cause came I unto this hour. Father, glorify thy name.

Understand this—these men had genuine reasons to be worried! And if we can be honest, they held up better than most of us would have! Nevertheless, focusing or meditating on the wrong things can negatively impact our mental, emotional, physical, and ultimately, our spiritual health. Howbeit, we all have problems—repeatedly! Job went on record saying this, "Man that is born of a woman is of few days, and full of trouble" (Job 14:1). In truth, you won't find anyone in the Bible who didn't face his or her fair share of worry, doubt, fear or anxiety. So, how do we not focus on the issues that threaten our peace every single day of our lives? The answer is in the Word!

	Steps	Scriptures
1	Focus on the Word and all that is positive in your life!	**Philippians 4:8:** Finally, brethren, whatsoever things are true, whatsoever things are honest, whatsoever things are just, whatsoever things are pure, whatsoever things are lovely,

Steps	Scriptures
	whatsoever things are of good report; if there be any virtue, and if there be any praise, think on these things.
2 Remember!	**Exodus 13:3:** And Moses said unto the people, Remember this day, in which ye came out from Egypt, out of the house of bondage; for by strength of hand the LORD brought you out from this place: there shall no leavened bread be eaten.
3 Be patient!	**Philippians 4:6-7:** Be careful for nothing; but in every thing by prayer and supplication with thanksgiving let your requests be made known unto God. And the peace of God, which passeth all understanding, shall keep your hearts and minds through Christ Jesus.
4 Praise God!	**Isaiah 61:3:** To appoint unto them that mourn in Zion, to give unto them beauty for ashes, the oil of joy for mourning, the garment of praise for the spirit of heaviness; that they might be called trees of righteousness, the planting of the LORD, that he might be glorified.
5 Do something about it!	**James 2:17:** Even so faith, if it hath not works, is dead, being alone.

Remember, God created meditation as a tool to assist us in growing our faith, but Satan has perverted the use of meditation so that he could grow his own fruits which, of course, are the works of the flesh. Your mind is the grounds where either the fruits of the Holy Spirit or the works (fruits) of the flesh will be planted and flourish. You get to determine which of these stay versus which will go. And please note that it is easy for a garden to become a field and eventually a forest if it's not tended to regularly.

MEDITATION MOMENT

The LORD is my light and my salvation; whom shall I fear? the LORD is the strength of my life; of whom shall I be afraid? When the wicked, even mine enemies and my foes, came upon me to eat up my flesh, they stumbled and fell. Though an host should encamp against me, my heart shall not fear: though war should rise against me, in this will I be confident. One thing have I desired of the LORD, that will I seek after; that I may dwell in the house of the LORD all the days of my life, to behold the beauty of the LORD, and to inquire in his temple. For in the time of trouble he shall hide me in his pavilion: in the secret of his tabernacle shall he hide me; he shall set me up upon a rock. And now shall mine head be lifted up above mine enemies round about me: therefore will I offer in his tabernacle sacrifices of joy; I will sing, yea, I will sing praises unto the LORD. Hear, O LORD, when I cry with my voice: have mercy also upon me, and answer me. When thou saidst, Seek ye my face; my heart said unto thee, Thy face, LORD, will I seek. Hide not thy face far from me; put not thy servant away in anger: thou hast been my help; leave me not, neither forsake me, O God of my salvation. When my father and my mother forsake me, then the LORD will take me up. Teach me thy way, O LORD, and lead me in a plain path, because of mine enemies. Deliver me not over unto the will of mine enemies: for false witnesses are risen up against me, and such as breathe out cruelty. I had fainted, unless I had believed to see the goodness of the LORD in the land of the living. Wait on the LORD: be of good courage, and he shall strengthen thine heart: wait, I say, on the LORD.

What are the meditation points for you? List them below.

More Meditation Points	
1	
2	
3	
4	
5	
6	
7	
8	

WORD STUDY

List the words that stand out to you and conduct a word study.
Again, if you don't have space in this document, use another document.

Word	
Definition or Etymology	

Word	
Definition or Etymology	

Word	
Definition or Etymology	

LET'S REFLECT!

_____

_____

_____

_____

_____

_____

_____

_____

_____

_____

_____

_____

_____

My Alarm Clock

Did You Know?
Humans have between four to six dreams per night, most of which are forgotten.

Did You Know?
Somniphobia is the fear of falling asleep.

Did You Know?
Sleep deprivation weakens the immune system.

Did You Know?
Women sleep more than men.

Did You Know?
Meditation helps lower our heart rate by igniting the parasympathetic nervous system; this encourages our bodies to breathe slower. Consequently, we get a better night's rest.

Using the boxes below, record the dates when you had trouble sleeping.
Did you meditate that night? Write yes or no in the box provided.

Monday	Tuesday	Wednesday	Thursday	Friday	Saturday	Sunday

THE ART OF REFLECTION

First and foremost, what is the difference between reflection and meditation?

Meditation takes a word from your mind to your heart.	Reflection takes a word from your heart to your mind.

Reflection (Etymology)
late 14c., reflexion, in reference to surfaces throwing back light or heat, from Late Latin reflexionem (nominative reflexio) "a reflection," literally "a bending back," noun of action from past participle stem of Latin reflectere "to bend back, bend backwards, turn away," from re- "back" (see re-) + flectere "to bend" (see flexible). Of the mind, from 1670s. Meaning "remark made after turning back one's thought on some subject" is from 1640s. Spelling with -ct- recorded from late 14c., established 18c., by influence of the verb.
Source: Online Etymology Dictionary

Our souls are the vaults of our thought life. In them, we store our memories, our beliefs, our desires, our secrets, and everything that it valuable to us. When all of these events and issues mix, they create what we call our belief systems. For example, a woman was raised by her negligent mother and her mother's abusive boyfriend. To add insult to injury, her biological father lived less than a mile away from her childhood home, and yet, he never came to visit, and whenever she visited him, he would rarely open the door. Whenever he did open the door, he would claim to be busy. Eventually, he got tired of trying to dodge her, so he told her that he was not her father. When the woman went to college, she was raped while attending a party for one of the local fraternities. Her experiences with men have always been chaotic, nevertheless, like most women, she still dreams of the day that she will marry and raise a family of her own. Her best friend is married to a great guy, so she has seen one or two positive examples of men. Her belief system would serve to marry all of her experiences and beliefs together to produce her reality and reproduce her mother's results. So, she may be a relatively nice woman, but until her mind has been changed, she will not make a good wife for any man. And while many of her experiences are no fault of her own, she still needs to address them and the thoughts, beliefs, habits and theories she's developed because of them. Think of it this way—that same woman meets a nice and relatively stable guy. The two get married and all seems well at first. That is, until the husband steps on one of his wife's triggers. He raises his voice at her ten-year old daughter … a daughter who is not biologically his. Remembering how condescending and narcissistic her stepfather was, she immediately begins to berate and belittle her husband. "She was using profanity," he says. "I was just correcting her." But the mother will not hear of it. "Don't worry about what she says!" shouts the mother. "That's my child and I'm the only one who can yell at her! You just need to mind your own business!" What happened here was she reflected on her childhood, remembered the abuse she'd suffered through and responded to that abuse. After a few arguments, the husband comes to realize that he has absolutely no say in how his wife raises her daughter, even though he is expected to stand in as the child's father both financially and morally. To keep the arguing down, he decides to avoid the child by staying in the couple's room whenever he comes home from work.

One day, the husband comes home from work early. The house is empty because his wife is at work and his stepdaughter is at school. He makes himself a sandwich and retreats to his bedroom. An hour later, he falls asleep. Three hours later, he is awakened by the sound of his bedroom door flinging open, coupled with the sound of his wife screaming at the top of her lungs. "Get out of my house!" she screams. Still groggy, the husband tries to make sense of his wife's anger. "What did I do now?" he says, wiping his eyes so that his vision could fully clear up. That's when he spots his stepdaughter standing in the doorway. Her arms are crossed, but her lips are moving. "Get out of my Momma's house!" she screams before being warned by her mother. "Go back to your room, baby! Momma got this!" She then snatches the cover off her husband. "Get up and get out of my house! I will put your stuff on the porch tonight, but I need you out of my house right now before I do something I'll regret!" The husband is relentless, however. "Okay," he says. "But first, I need to know what I did wrong!" After this, he hears the story. As it turns out, his ten-year old stepdaughter accidentally left her house keys at the house that day. When she returned home from school, she was relieved to see her stepfather's car in the driveway, but that relief turned to devastation when the stepfather didn't open the door after she'd knocked for about twenty minutes. Frustrated, the young girl called her mother at work. The mother then had to take off early to come and let her daughter in the house. Who's wrong here? The mother is, of course! The problem is, she is still responding to her childhood trauma, and she's using her husband as a fill-in for her father and stepfather.

Again, your soul is the vault of your thought-life. You cannot pull anything from that vault that hasn't been stored in it. This is the goal of meditation; that is to take a thought and bring it into the mind until it makes its way into the subconscious (heart). The goal of reflection, on the other hand, is to take what has been stored and bring it back to the forefront of your mind. For example, as believers, we should be meditating on the Word of God. We should also reflect on what we have learned, after all, the objective of gathering biblical information is not centered around knowing what God said, but understanding and applying it. It is also centered around building and growing our relationship with God!

Understanding Reflection

The first question that most people ask is, "What is reflection?" Think about your reflection in a mirror. What you see is what you present to the world, but how you see yourself does not necessarily determine how the world sees you. For example, we have all seen those women who wear entirely too much makeup. And to add insult to injury, we've all seen the ones who didn't properly blend their makeup, which caused them to look like they were wearing masks. We've seen women who've overdrawn their eyebrows, put on too much lipstick or put on too much eyeliner. And we've all asked ourselves, "Does she have a mirror at home?" And of course, the answer is yes. She has a mirror and a reflection, but how she sees herself and how we see her are not necessarily one and the same. If she is ever going to change, she would need to reflect, but first, she has to have something to reflect on. What this means is, she will need to know the right way in order for her to identify that there is a wrong way. In other words, she needs something to compare her results to. If she, for example, meets a professional MUA (makeup artist) and starts studying her work and style, she could potentially learn the proper way to apply her makeup. And this wouldn't be an overnight victory, but eventually, she'd become better at crafting her gift or skill. For example, one day, she may find herself applying her makeup when, all of a sudden, she realizes that her lipstick application looks nothing like her favorite MUA's applications. In that moment, she begins to reflect on the artist's work, and that's when she'll change how she applies her lipstick. This is one small victory, but if she continues, she will eventually become skilled at what she does. This is the art of reflection. The goal of reflection can be summed up in one word—growth! Let me explain.

In the world of meditation, reflection is often misused because it encourages people to remember or reflect on specific events or incidents so that the person could learn from the experience. And while this sounds great, it does little to help with healing the person. How so? People reflect all the time, but most of their reflecting is negative. For example, if you step outside your apartment complex and ask your not-so-respectful neighbor to stop parking in your parking space, chances are, he'll file the incident away in his subconscious as an offense, and consequently, he will see you as his enemy, even though he was wrong and you asked him kindly to move his car. So, two years later when he sees you outside attempting to start your car, he'll proudly pass you by because he can't stop reflecting on the moment you offended him. But what if I told you that this is all he knows? Vengeance is a lifestyle for him, after all, he was raised by vengeful parents, grew up in a community where vengeance was a part of the culture, and his entire world has been shaped by vengeful thinking. So, how would reflection help him? It wouldn't; that is, unless he finally learned another way to view rebuke and another approach to process his offenses. The point is, while reflection can be a healthy tool, it can and oftentimes is used in the wrong way. So, again, what is reflection? "Reflection is concerned with consciously looking at and thinking about our experiences, actions, feelings, and responses, and then interpreting or analyzing them in order to learn from them" (Atkins and Murphy, 1994; Boud et al., 1994). The two goals of reflection are interpretation and analysis (inspection).

Interpretation

Reflection can be a life-changing and life-saving tool if we interpret the scriptures and our experiences from a healthy, Godly perspective. A great example of this can be found in the story of Job. Let's preview the onset of Job's pain.

Job 1:1-12

There was a man in the land of Uz, whose name was Job; and that man was perfect and upright, and one that feared God, and eschewed evil. And there were born unto him seven sons and three daughters. His substance also was seven thousand sheep, and three thousand camels, and five hundred yoke of oxen, and five hundred she asses, and a very great household; so that this man was the greatest of all the men of the east. And his sons went and feasted in their houses, every one his day; and sent and called for their three sisters to eat and to drink with them. And it was so, when the days of their feasting were gone about, that Job sent and sanctified them, and rose up early in the morning, and offered burnt offerings according to the number of them all: for Job said, It may be that my sons have sinned, and cursed God in their hearts. Thus did Job continually.

Now there was a day when the sons of God came to present themselves before the LORD, and Satan came also among them. And the LORD said unto Satan, Whence comest thou? Then Satan answered the LORD, and said, From going to and fro in the earth, and from walking up and down in it. And the LORD said unto Satan, Hast thou considered my servant Job, that there is none like him in the earth, a perfect and an upright man, one that feareth God, and escheweth evil? Then Satan answered the LORD, and said, Doth Job fear God for nought? Hast not thou made an hedge about him, and about his house, and about all that he hath on every side? thou hast blessed the work of his hands, and his substance is increased in the land. But put forth thine hand now, and touch all that he hath, and he will curse thee to thy face. And the LORD said unto Satan, Behold, all that he hath is in thy power; only upon himself put not forth thine hand. So Satan went forth from the presence of the LORD.

Job was a perfect man, and by "perfect," the scripture isn't saying that he was blameless, but it literally means that he trusted God. Of course, our faith in God is often revealed in our lifestyles and the fruits that manifest themselves in our lives. As a matter of fact, the men of old measured one another's relationships with God by looking at several factors, including wealth and health. If a man prospered, was healthy and had sound, healthy and moral children, he was seen as a man of great faith, a blessed man and a man of integrity. On the other hand, if a man was poor and if he himself or one of his children were sickly, he was seen as an unclean and immoral man. This is why the disciples of Jesus, upon coming across a blind man, asked Him, "Master, who did sin, this man, or his parents, that he was born blind?" All the same, when Satan attacked Job, his friends began to question his relationship with God. They believed that Job had been living a life contrary to the one he professed. Consequently, Job found himself defending his faith and his integrity, but the questions, the accusations and the assumptions slowly began to take a toll on Job's already ailing mental health. Before long, he found himself questioning the very meaning of life. In Job 38 and 39, God speaks up, and the first thing that He does is rebuke Job for his wrongful interpretation of Him. Why is this important to note? Because Job, like many of us, found himself in a storm, and when this happened, he began to reflect on his life and his relationship with God. But part of reflection is interpretation, and a wrongful interpretation can and always does lead to a wrongful perspective of God (a misunderstanding). Misunderstanding is the very fabric that false religions are made of.

Consider the word "correction." To get a better understanding of it, consider the fact that Lucifer's body had been made with timbrels and pipes, and it was covered in precious jewels. Every time Lucifer had a vain imagination or another meeting with God's angels in the darkness, his pipes would twist and bend all the more. Another word for "twisted" is perverted. Correction would look like God bending Lucifer's pipes back into place, but of course, this didn't happen. Nevertheless, God promised to do this for those of us who chose to reconcile with Him through our faith and relationship with Jesus Christ. So, when God corrects us, He is literally putting pressure on our perversion; the goal is to bend our minds back into the shape He created them in, so that we'll see and serve Him for who He is! He is literally bending us back into shape. This is so that we can reflect on all the good He has done for us and get to know Him for who He is, and not through the perverted prisms that religion has caused us to view Him through. This the role and goal of interpretation.

Analysis (Inspection)

Google's Online Dictionary defines "analyze" this way: "examine methodically and in detail the constitution or structure of (something, especially information), typically for purposes of explanation and interpretation."

Analysis is a huge and important part of reflection because how you analyze a thing will determine:

1. The interpretation you come out of it with.

2. How you introduce it to others.

Think of analysis this way. Two cars collide on a highway, and thankfully, none of the passengers are injured in the accident. Two highway patrolmen arrive to access the accident and write up a report. Driver A says that the accident was the fault of Driver B, but Driver B claims that the accident was totally Driver A's fault. No witnesses have stopped to collaborate either man's story, so the officers have to rely on their training and what they see. And it is hard to ascertain who's telling the truth because both cars are now resting on the shoulder of the highway, so after a careful examination, the officers decide to give both drivers a ticket. Driver A retains a lawyer and so does Driver B, but Driver B is suing for over $100 thousand, claiming that his vehicle was totaled, plus, one day after the accident, he had to be hospitalized for back pain. He's suing Driver A's insurance carrier for the price to replace his vehicle, medical bills, lost wages (since he could not return to work for one month) and pain and suffering. Driver A, on the other hand, is just suing for $10 thousand to fix the dent in his car, replace his bumper, get a new paint job and for loss of wages. After careful consideration and deliberation, the judge decides that Driver A is at fault, and in another proceeding, Driver B is awarded $100 thousand to Driver A's chagrin. How did the judge come to this conclusion? The lawyers put in all of the investigative work, of course. They each hired investigators to analyze the pictures, the police report and each man's account of the accident, and they found that Driver A had admittedly:
1. Had an argument with his wife that morning, and she'd demanded that he leave their marital home.
2. Just left a bar where he'd consumed two alcoholic beverages, and while he'd barely passed the breathalyzer test, he was still relatively tipsy.
3. Tried to leave the scene of the crime, but his attempts had been thwarted by the woman who'd been riding in the car with him.

They also discovered that:
1. The paint from his bumper had been found on the plaintiff's vehicle, and it was upon impact that his bumper broke off of his car.
2. He was arguing with the woman in the car and trying to take her phone from her when he'd lost control of his vehicle.
3. He had two prior DUI's on his record.

This great investigative work helped Driver B to win his judgment. But the work itself is what we call analysis or inspection. And hear me—when dealing with the American Judicial System, a lawyer has to carefully examine all the evidence, use his or her knowledge about the court system, the judge who's trying the case and his or her client's criminal backgrounds in order to build a solid case. One slip-up can cost him or her the case.

Let's look at another example in 1 Kings 3.

1 Kings 3:16-28 (ESV)
Then two prostitutes came to the king and stood before him. The one woman said, "Oh, my lord, this woman and I live in the same house, and I gave birth to a child while she was in the house. Then on the third day after I gave birth, this woman also gave birth. And we were alone. There was no one else with us in the house; only we two were in the house. And this woman's son died in the night, because she lay on him. And she arose at midnight and took my son from beside me, while your servant slept, and laid him at her breast, and laid her dead son at my breast. When I rose in the morning to nurse my child, behold, he was dead. But when I looked at him closely in the morning, behold, he was not the child that I had borne." But the other woman said, "No, the living child is mine, and the dead child is yours." The first said, "No, the dead child is yours, and the living child is mine." Thus they spoke before the king. Then the king said, "The one says, 'This is my son that is alive, and your son is dead'; and the other says, 'No; but your son is dead, and my son is the living one.'" And the king said, "Bring me a sword." So a sword was brought before the king. And the king said, "Divide the living child in two, and give half to the one and half to the other." Then the woman whose son was alive said to the king, because her heart yearned for her son, "Oh, my lord, give her the living child, and by no means put him to death." But the other said, "He shall be neither mine nor yours; divide him." Then the king answered and said, "Give the living child to the first woman, and by no means put him to death; she is his mother." And all Israel heard of the judgment that the king had rendered, and they stood in awe of the king, because they perceived that the wisdom of God was in him to do justice.

This was one of Solomon's crowning moments! This was a moment when the people began to trust in his leadership. But did Solomon analyze the evidence? Yes and no. There was no crime scene to examine and there was no physical evidence that could be examined, so Solomon had to rely on the wisdom of God. A leader ahead of his time, he analyzed the countenances and the responses of both women. In short, he used what we now call psychology. He said to his servants, "Divide the living child in two!" Hear me—the command had gone forth! The servant who had been given the charge didn't know that it was just a test, and like Abraham had done with his son, Isaac, the servant had gone forth and was about to slaughter the child. This was an intense moment! Every millisecond behind that command was sheer torment! The mother's heart began to melt within her, but the other woman didn't have too much time to craft up another lie, so in that very sensitive, adrenaline-fueled and paralyzing moment, the mother of the child did what any (sound) mother would do. She put her child before herself. "No!" she yelled out, watching the servant raise his sword. "Please don't kill him! Just give him to her!" She'd decided to watch him grow up from a distance, thinking that another woman was his mother. She'd decided that the best way to protect her son was to sacrifice her own desires to nurture and raise him. But in that moment, the other woman hadn't had much time to think of an answer... one that would make her appear to be the mother. She'd only rehearsed for a standard court appearance, but this was in no ways the standard of Israel. No other king had ever commanded that a child be put to death. So, her envy spoke up on her behalf. "Yeah, divide him in two! That'll fix the problem!" she shouted. Because the problem wasn't that she missed her child; the problem was, she didn't want her roommate to have a child if she didn't have one. But after analyzing their response to negative stimuli, King Solomon was able to ascertain that the grieved woman was the true mother, so he commanded that her son be returned to her. Isn't this what happened when God created Heaven and Earth, and darkness had been upon the face of the waters? God looked at the darkness, a matter completely antithetical to who He is, and said, "Let there be light." In other words, let there be revelation. Let the darkness give up its secrets! In other words, God began to address everything that did not look like Him or reflect His nature!

How can we relate this to reflective meditating? It's simple. Every thought should be tried; another word for tried is tested. All the same, every incident, conversation and belief should be carefully examined; this is what helps us with our interpretation of an event, a scripture, etc. In short, the goal of analysis is so that we can extract revelation from every thought, every scripture and everything that we expose ourselves to. Consider this—most of the people who've walked out of your life did so because of a misunderstanding. They simply misinterpreted something you said or over-analyzed something you did, or vice versa. Maybe, you were the culprit behind the breakup, the failed friendship or the family drama. Maybe, you misinterpreted someone's words or choices, and consequently, you berated that person, and now, that individual is but a distant memory. This is what happens when we don't properly analyze, not just the situation at hand, but our own hearts. If we can be honest, many of the fights we've had with loved ones stemmed from the fact that we were having a bad day. Analyzing or inspecting the events of our lives helps us to mature, make better choices and not sabotage covenant relationships. Please note that the opposite of inspect is blame. This is when we try to analyze other people and their choices, all the while, turning a blind eye to our own issues.

Dark Reflections

Space is an interesting place. It is a dimension filled with black matter (darkness), and spaced throughout this darkness, you will find stars and other galactic bodies. Scientists have long studied the phenomena that is space, and one of the questions that many scientists have attempted to answer is, "Why is space black, especially given the fact that it's filled with so many light bodies?" And of course, there have been theories upon theories drafted, but no laws have been established, meaning, this is a mystery that is still unanswered. One of those theories (actually regarded as a paradox, which means it contradicts an already established theory) is Olbers' Paradox. It also means that it's more of a question or a casting of doubt than a theory. Let's look at its meaning.

Olber's Paradox
In cosmology, paradox relating to the problem of why the sky is dark at night. If the universe is endless and uniformly populated with luminous stars, then every line of sight must eventually terminate at the surface of a star. Hence, contrary to observation, this argument implies that the night sky should everywhere be bright, with no dark spaces between the stars. This paradox was discussed in 1823 by the German astronomer Heinrich Wilhelm Olbers, and its discovery is widely attributed to him. The problem was considered by earlier investigators and can be traced back to Johannes Kepler, who, in 1610, advanced it as an argument against the notion of a limitless universe containing an infinite number of stars. Various resolutions have been proposed at different times. If the assumptions are accepted, then the simplest resolution is that the average luminous lifetime of stars is far too short for light to have yet reached the Earth from very distant stars. In the context of an expanding universe, it can be argued similarly: the universe is too young for light to have reached the Earth from very distant regions.

Source: Encyclopedia Britannica

In a nutshell, the universally accepted theory regarding space is that it is an infinite, timeless and static space. Infinite, meaning, it is without ends or impossible to measure. Timeless, meaning, it has no age or no start; instead, it has always existed. And static, meaning, it is set in place; it does not move, but is stationary. Olber's Paradox has gotten a lot of attention and traction in the scientific community, but again, it still doesn't establish facts or laws. It just raises a few questions. And while scientists struggle to establish theories regarding space, let's establish a few (spiritual) theories and paradoxes of our own to better understand what we are seeing. A better way to say this is, what we are witnessing. But because I cannot officially establish some of what I'm about to propose as theories or laws, I will start off some statements or theories that I have with "What if..."

Revelation 12:1-4: And there appeared a great wonder in heaven; a woman clothed with the sun, and the moon under her feet, and upon her head a crown of twelve stars: And she being

97

with child cried, travailing in birth, and pained to be delivered. And there appeared another wonder in heaven; and behold a great red dragon, having seven heads and ten horns, and seven crowns upon his heads. And his tail drew the third part of the stars of heaven, and did cast them to the earth: and the dragon stood before the woman which was ready to be delivered, for to devour her child as soon as it was born.

We've already established that the third part of the stars that Satan's tail drew were angels. This is why demons are referred to as "fallen angels." Remember that the angels followed Lucifer into the darkness where he began to slander the name and character of God. But before I can propose anything, let's look at the three dimensions of Heaven.

Third Heaven	Second Heaven	First Heaven
God's Throne	Outer Space	Atmospheric (Sky)

Revelation 12:7-9: And there was war in heaven: Michael and his angels fought against the dragon; and the dragon fought and his angels, and prevailed not; neither was their place found any more in heaven. And the great dragon was cast out, that old serpent, called the Devil, and Satan, which deceiveth the whole world: he was cast out into the earth, and his angels were cast out with him.

Revelation 12:13: And when the dragon saw that he was cast unto the earth, he persecuted the woman which brought forth the man child.

What if the stars that we see crowning our night sky are really fallen spirits? What if the dragon (Satan) being cast unto the Earth didn't necessarily mean he was cast "into" the Earth? What if Satan got into the Earth by entering a snake, but he really wanted a human body to inhabit? What if Satan's temptation of Eve wasn't just centered around getting her into sin, but it was more of his attempt to hijack her body? What if Eve became the first demon-possessed soul on the face of this planet? What if after she seduced Adam to sin, Adam found himself in need of deliverance as well? What if what we see in the night sky are really angels (demons) that have been cast into utter darkness? Would this then explain why most stars are one to three billion miles apart? In other words, most of them cannot help or draw strength from one another. Again, these are just questions. What if astrology was revelation in reverse? In other words, it teaches man to relate to darkness, instead of teaching man to relate to God. What if it is false revelation designed to create a portal between the demonic kingdom and the kingdom of man? Needless to say, outside of the many questions and theories that we can muster up, one thing is for sure and that is—YAHWEH has rescued us from the kingdom of darkness and delivered us to the Kingdom of His dear Son, Jesus Christ. In other words, neither Satan nor his angels have any (legal) right to hold us in bondage; that is, unless we transfer our authority (power) to them. And of course, the kingdom of darkness will stop at no ends to find human bodies to inhabit, and their auditions to enter into our hearts and lives often comes through a series of commercials called imaginations. Imaginations take place in the soul which, of course, is comprised of the mind, will and emotions. The soul, of course, is the second dimension of our being. Look at the chart below to see how this compares to each level of Heaven.

Body	Soul	Spirit
First Heaven	Second Heaven	Third Heaven
Egypt	Wilderness	Promised Land

The body can be compared to the first Heaven because the first Heaven is the natural atmosphere in the Earth's realm. It can be seen; it can be felt and it can be altered. The spirit, on the other hand, can be compared to the third Heaven. It is the space where God dwells; the space that we have little to no power over. But for this presentation, we are focusing on the soul which, of course, can be compared to the second Heaven (outer space). In the soul, we find our mind, will and emotions. This is an infinite space filled with unimaginable potential; it's also littered with thoughts and beliefs that have yet to be cast down. In the highest level of our souls (our minds) is the faculty in which our imaginations take place. As we discussed earlier, our imaginations are a series of images (some still, some animated) that interrupt our day-to-day lives. We welcome some of our imaginations, we tolerate some of our imaginations and some imaginations can be downright tormenting. Nevertheless, as broad as the sphere of the mind can be, we have full control of it. Needless to say, however, there are a lot of people who feel like they don't have control over what takes place in their heads; this is because they've allowed the muscles of their minds (their wills) to become weak. This typically happens when people subject themselves to a lot of ungodly images and sounds (media). Over time, as they develop a more intimate relationship with God, they began to fill their mental space with scriptures, as well as positive images and sounds. But this does not replace what's already stored in the memory bank; it simply serves to accompany it. So, they are constantly finding themselves dealing with dark imaginations—some of them are stored in the soul, while others are completely demonic.

There are three types of dark reflections. They are:
- Dark Memories (Traumas)
- Vain Imaginations
- Fears

Dark Memories (Traumas)	Vain Imaginations	Fears
Past	Present	Future
Remember, there are two levels of the soul that store trauma. They are the subconscious and unconscious mind. The unconscious mind stores forgotten trauma, whereas the subconscious stores the traumas we remember. These imaginations are nothing but replays of a traumatic event that took place in our lives.	Vain imaginations are useless or unprofitable thoughts that invade our head-space. These imaginations were triggered by either a traumatic event or an unpleasant event. They can be fantasies about the future that we've stored in our minds; these are thoughts that we regularly reflect on, meaning, we bring them back to the conscious mind from time-to-time, especially when we've been triggered.	Our fears stem from several places, including (but not limited to) dark memories, vain imaginations, foolish conversations and media. Fears are oftentimes futuristic because many of them serve as false warnings of something that is to come or could potentially come if we don't perform a certain action. This is why the Bible tells us to take no thought for tomorrow.

Hear me—the mind was not created to be filled with darkness! Again, the soul is like the second Heaven. Our goal is to catch and cast down every unprofitable and vain imagination. The goal is to take our thoughts out of Egypt and bring them to the Promised Land. But how do we do this? We have to lead our minds or imaginations out of Egypt, through the wilderness and into the Promised Land. What this looks like is simply changing our diet from Egyptian food to manna, and eventually to spiritual food.

Egypt	Wilderness	Promised Land
Slaves	Servants	Sons

Egypt

Once we have been saved and we've made the exodus from damnation to salvation, we then have to study to show ourselves approved. Of course, this means that we have to study the Word of God and not just the scriptures. What does this mean? Anyone can study the black and white letters on the pages of our Bibles, but not everyone has welcomed the Spirit of God to give them understanding of what they are reading. In other words, we have to go from having a relationship with God to having an intimate relationship with Him. In short, our goal is to grow from being slaves to sons.

Galatians 4:1-7

Now I say, That the heir, as long as he is a child, differeth nothing from a servant, though he be lord of all; but is under tutors and governors until the time appointed of the father. Even so we, when we were children, were in bondage under the elements of the world: But when the fullness of the time was come, God sent forth his Son, made of a woman, made under the law, to redeem them that were under the law, that we might receive the adoption of sons. And because ye are sons, God hath sent forth the Spirit of his Son into your hearts, crying, Abba, Father. Wherefore thou art no more a servant, but a son; and if a son, then an heir of God through Christ.

Again, we apply this to our thought-life by:
1. Getting planted in a good church.
2. Studying the Word of God (consistently).
3. Getting therapy (if needed).
4. Changing the channel on our television and our radios.

The goal here is to quench and ultimately eliminate our desires for the things of the world. Hear me—you can't complain about what's taking place in your mind if you are not careful about what you expose yourself to! A lot of what takes place in our imaginations is nothing but our souls vomiting up what it's been fed.

Wilderness

At this stage, we're more mature; our minds have been developed more, and we've learned a few scriptures here and there. Nevertheless, we are still led by our emotions. This is the outer space of our mental and emotional development! This is the puberty stage of our development! This is the time when we have to be more intentional about what we consume (mentally and emotionally). All the same, this is the time when we need leaders who aren't afraid of us! We need mentors (tutors and governors) who will customize a diet for us so that we can reach our full potential in Christ. Sadly enough, it is at this stage of development that most believers fall, meaning, they give up. They don't necessarily return to Egypt; they simply make their beds and dig their graves in the wilderness. In other words, they stop fighting dark reflections and everything that takes place in their minds, and they learn to live with their issues.

At this stage, we need:
1. More accountability.
2. To serve (at our local churches and other events).
3. To increase our study and worship time.

4. To fast often!
5. More therapy (if needed).

Getting control over our mental and emotional health is more than us forcing ourselves to think positive thoughts! We need reinforcements! We need mentors, books, schedules and accountability!

Promised Land

Before Joshua led the Israelites into the Promised Land, he had to first prepare them for war. They were going to have to drive out the inhabitants of the land. This represents deliverance. In truth, every believer should submit to deliverance every quarter; that is, about four times a year. This is because we lose some of the mental battles that we find ourselves in. Sometimes, we give in to unforgiveness. Sometimes, we give in to vengeful thoughts. We may even give in to lustful thoughts. Sometimes, we just get weary and stop fighting back. So, before and after we enter the Promised Land (our callings), we should have a diet replete with study time, accountability and deliverance.

Over the years, we've just been taught to think positive thoughts. Nowadays, you'll find people meditating on positive words and affirmations, and while I'm not against this, it simply isn't enough. The muscle of the mind is too strong to be trained by mere thoughts when it's been bent out of shape by choices! In other words, you can't mentally undo what you physically did! That's like eating fast food every day, and then trying to think yourself skinny. Dark matter or dark reflections aren't just the products of bad thoughts; they are oftentimes the products of bad choices! Many people have asked, "Why is space black, especially given the fact that it's filled with so many light bodies?" All the same, you may find yourself asking a similar question— "Why are my thoughts dark, even though I'm Christian?" The answer is—the mind, as infinite of a space as it may be, is not static. Unlike the space above our planet, our minds can be changed; they can be transformed, but this happens only when the mind is renewed. Again, the mind is renewed through:

Bible Study	Accountability	Mentorship
Study (Books)	Media	Relationships (Plantonic)
Prayer	Self Denial (Fasting)	Deliverance

Laws of Reflection

James 1:22-25: But be ye doers of the word, and not hearers only, deceiving your own selves. For if any be a hearer of the word, and not a doer, he is like unto a man beholding his natural face in a glass: For he beholdeth himself, and goeth his way, and straightway forgetteth what manner of man he was. But whoso looketh into the perfect law of liberty, and continueth therein, he being not a forgetful hearer, but a doer of the work, this man shall be blessed in his deed.

In the aforementioned scripture, the glass that the man saw himself through, of course, was a mirror. And of course, mirrors back then were quite different than the ones we have today, but they served the same purpose. They allowed people to look at themselves so that they could see themselves before presenting themselves to the world. Mirrors reverse the images in front of them and cast what we call a reflection. Before we go deeper into this lesson, check out this article from Live Science about the history of mirrors.

Who Invented the Mirror?

The silvered-glass mirrors found throughout the world today first got their start in Germany almost 200 years ago.

In 1835, German chemist Justus von Liebig developed a process for applying a thin layer of metallic silver to one side of a pane of clear glass. This technique was soon adapted and improved upon, allowing for the mass production of mirrors.

Modern mirrors may have originated in the 19th century, but mirrors in general have actually been around for much longer. According to a 2006 review by vision scientist Dr. Jay Enoch in the journal Optometry and Vision Science, people in Anatolia — modern-day Turkey — manufactured the first mirrors out of ground and polished obsidian (volcanic glass) about 8,000 years ago. Mirrors made of polished copper later popped up in Mesopotamia (now Iraq) and Egypt from 4000 to 3000 B.C. About 1,000 years later, people in Central and South America began making mirrors out of polished stone, while Chinese and Indian mirror makers crafted them out of bronze.

In the first century A.D., the Roman author Pliny the Elder alludes to the first recorded use of glass mirrors in his encyclopedia Natural History, but the mirrors apparently never came into general use at the time.

Though different cultures independently created reflective mirrors at various times throughout history, nature should perhaps be crowned as the true inventor of the looking glass. "The very first mirrors most probably were quiet pools of water and rock or clay containers of water," wrote Enoch. Of course, these natural mirrors pale in comparison to the manufactured mirrors of today.

But not everyone in the world has welcomed the introduction of mirrors. When an anthropologist introduced mirrors to the isolated Biami people of Papua New Guinea in the 1970s, the tribe reportedly met their eerie reflections with terror, rather than fascination.

Source: Live Science/ Who Invented the Mirror/ Joseph Castro

Again, the idea or concept of mirrors is over eight thousand years old. There are several biblical references to mirrors, with the most notable mention being found in the book of Exodus. Moses had received the command from the Lord to build what is now known as the Tabernacle of Moses. Before doing this, the Israelites were required to give up several of their personal items to aid in building the Tabernacle. Exodus 38:8 talks about the creation of the Brazen Laver; it reads, "And he made the laver of brass, and the foot of it of brass, of the looking glasses of the women assembling, which assembled at the door of the tabernacle of the congregation." In short, the Hebrew women had to give up their mirrors, and these mirrors were used to create the Brazen Laver. The Brazen Laver was a basin that the priests used to wash their hands and feet before entering and exiting the Holy Place. Before entering the Holy Place, the priests had to make a sacrifice for themselves; this represented salvation before service. One of the laws of Reflection is:

> **You cannot change what you refuse to see.**

The Brazen Laver not only presented them with the opportunity to wash their hands and their feet, but before the water was stirred, the priests could look into the water and see themselves. They could see their reflections. Before they attempted to remove the speck from the eyes of the congregation, they first had to clean themselves up. This required them to see themselves.

What is a reflection?
- Reflection is a serious thought or consideration.
- Reflection is meditation in reverse. Meditation takes the Word of God from your intellect to your heart. Reflection takes what's in your heart and brings it to your mind.
- Reflection is the throwing back by a body or surface of light, heat, or sound.
- Reflection is an image seen in a mirror.
- Reflection is a theme that is a consequence of or arises from something else.

Genesis 1:1-2: In the beginning God created the heaven and the earth. And the earth was without form, and void; and darkness was upon the face of the deep. And the Spirit of God moved upon the face of the waters.

Before God created Heaven and Earth, there were no raw materials for Him to create them with, so out of Himself, He pulled Heaven and Earth. So, just like David would go down to the river to see his reflection, in the beginning, God began to move over the face of the waters, and what did He see? His reflection!

Genesis 1:9: And God said, Let the waters under the heaven be gathered together unto one place, and let the dry land appear: and it was so.

Again, in the beginning, God pulled Heaven and Earth out of Himself. Who is God?

Front of God	Back of God
Alpha	Omega
Beginning	End
Genesis	Revelation
Abba (Father)	Jesus (Son)

He is the Beginning and the End! So, God pulled Heaven and Earth out of Himself! And what He saw when He hovered over the waters was His own reflection; in other words, He saw what was inside of Himself! He saw untapped potential! When He pulled Heaven and Earth out of Himself, He then pulled mankind out of one of the materials found in the Earth and, of course, that is dust. After this, He pulled Eve out of Adam, and He pulled Cain, Abel, and Seth out of Eve! Hear me—another law of reflection says:

> **You cannot take something out of someone else that you can't first take out of yourself!**

Remember what Jesus said in Matthew 7:4-5. "Or how wilt thou say to thy brother, Let me pull out the mote out of thine eye; and, behold, a beam is in thine own eye? Thou hypocrite, first cast out the beam out of thine own eye; and then shalt thou see clearly to cast out the mote out of thy brother's eye." Let's look closer at the word "hypocrite."

Hypocrite (Definition)
One who, like a stage-player, feigns to be what he is not. The epithet is generally applied to

those who assume the appearance of virtue or piety, without possessing the reality. Our Savior accused the Pharisees of hypocrisy, Luke 12:1.

Source: ATS Bible Dictionary

Hypocrite (Definition)

One who puts on a mask and feigns himself to be what he is not; a dissembler in religion. Our Lord severely rebuked the scribes and Pharisees for their hypocrisy (Matthew 6:2, 5, 16). "The hypocrite's hope shall perish" (Job 8:13). The Hebrew word here rendered "hypocrite" rather means the "godless" or "profane," as it is rendered in Jeremiah 23:11, i.e., polluted with crimes.

Source: Easton's Bible Dictionary

The Greek word for "hypocrite" is "hupokrités", and it literally means: "One who answers, an actor, a hypocrite." It means to wear a mask or operate under false pretenses. In other words, to cast a false reflection. So, one of the most important goals and roles of reflection is to keep you from becoming a hypocrite! Consider what Lucifer did—he defamed God's name and His character in the dark, but when he came out of the darkness, he worshiped the Lord in the presence of the angels. But because his pipes had been bent by the darkness (very high concentrations of dark matter causes light to bend, and Lucifer was the Light-Bearer), because his timbrels and his tabrets were twisted, the sounds he emitted revealed his deepest, darkest secret. He didn't sound the same; he didn't even look the same! He probably sounded like a man with a hangover, asking, "Why is it so bright in here?" Not realizing that anytime you are in perpetual darkness, the sudden emergence of light will always hurt your eyes. This is why God, in His wisdom, incorporated what we call dusk and dawn; these are the gradual processes of going from darkness to light or from light to darkness. This allows our eyes to adjust to each setting.

Another aspect or dimension of reflection is inspection. Let's look at Genesis 2:19. "And out of the ground the LORD God formed every beast of the field, and every fowl of the air; and brought them unto Adam to see what he would call them: and whatsoever Adam called every living creature, that was the name thereof." When you are reflecting on a thought, an idea, a conversation, or a problem, what you're doing is inspecting it. What God did was brought all of the animals to Adam. Why did He do this? So that Adam could inspect them! To inspect means to look over or to examine. The law of inspection allowed Adam to inspect and adequately name the animals. What was he doing? He was reflecting or echoing what God had already called them. Understand this—another word for inspection is representation. If you are a good reflection of God, you are a good representation of Him. This brings us to another law of reflection—one that we all have heard; that is:

Imitation is the sincerest form of flattery.

This is why God told us, "Be ye holy, for I am holy." In this, He is simply saying, "Follow my lead. Imitate my ways. Be like me." In short, our job is to be pure enough to reflect the light of the Son! This is so that the world can get light. If we are full of perversion and ungodly ideologies, we'll only absorb the light when it comes to us. This is why Ephesians 5:8-11 says, "For ye were sometimes darkness, but now are ye light in the Lord: walk as children of light: (For the fruit of the Spirit is in all goodness and righteousness and truth;) proving what is acceptable unto the Lord. And have no fellowship with the unfruitful works of darkness, but rather reprove them." Hear me—it takes light to reflect light! For example, dark colored clothes absorb light. It then converts this light into heat. This is why it is not a great idea to wear dark clothes in the summer. Remember, Lucifer met with the angels of God in the darkness. Another fact worth mentioning is—reflections are caused by light bouncing off an object. The way that this works is, whenever light waves hit a surface that does not absorb the energy, if the surface is smooth and shiny, the light will bounce the light off of it, thus, producing an image or, better yet, a reflection. The point is, Lucifer met the angels in darkness because his body was made of precious gems, all of which reflected the light of God. But remember, the Bible tells us that darkness doesn't comprehend light. So, in the darkness, there was no light to bounce off his body. Nevertheless, the light he'd absorbed by God did shine, but it did not illuminate the darkness. (This is the same effect we see in the night sky. The stars cover the sky, but they don't illuminate it.) In the darkness, he didn't cast God's reflection. He was able to establish his own separate identity, thus separating himself or distinguishing himself from God. And while the angels knew that he wasn't God, he was made in such a way that he would only radiate the beauty of holiness (God), meaning, even though he would stand before the congregation, all the angels saw was God radiating through him. But according to the scriptures, he became lifted up (prideful) because of his beauty. Nevertheless, in the darkness, he didn't worry about God inspecting him. In the darkness, he was able to disguise himself as an angel of light when, in truth, he'd become a dark angel. Howbeit, in all of his knowledge of God, what he didn't know is that God is all-knowing; there is nothing hidden from God, since He is Light, and remember, Lucifer was supposed to be His Light-Bearer or, better yet, reflection. This is why Luke 8:17 tells us, "For nothing is secret, that shall not be made manifest; neither any thing hid, that shall not be known and come abroad." In summary, Lucifer essentially quit his job as Light-Bearer so that he could establish his own brand—one that was independent from God and all that He represents.

In the times of old, there were what we now refer to as Schools of the Prophets. Why were these schools needed? 1 Corinthians 14:32. It reads, "And the spirits of the prophets are subject to the prophets."

Schools of the Prophets
"(1 Sam. 19:18-24; 2 Kings 2:3, 5, 7, 12, 15) were instituted for" the purpose of training young men for the prophetical and priestly offices. (See [553] PROPHET; [554] SAMUEL.)
Source: King James Bible Online

The Law of Reflection was why these concentrated companies like the Schools of the Prophets were created. Proverbs 27:17 reads, "Iron sharpeneth iron; so a man sharpeneth the countenance of his friend." Hear me—another law of reflection is:

You can only be sharpened by people who have been built by the same substance as you!

If someone is not equally matched or yoked with you, or that person does not outrank you, he or she cannot make you better! Think of it this way—if you release light, you need someone to bounce it off of. Of course, light represents revelation. This is why Elisha had to be raised up by Elijah. This is why the Prophet Samuel had to be raised by the Prophet Eli. Every man needed to see a reflection of his future or a reflection of his potential, either good or bad. In Elisha's case, he saw what he could potentially become, which was a mighty prophet of God. In Samuel's case, he saw what he could potentially become if he didn't steward the office of the prophet correctly.

Reflection: the act of reflecting, as in casting back a light or heat, mirroring, or giving back or showing an image; the state of being reflected in this way.
(Source: Dictionary.com)

The Tabernacle of Moses was a three-dimensional structure, complete with an Outer Court, Inner Court, and the Holy of Holies. Outside of the Tabernacle, you first encountered the door. As you walked through the door, you then encountered the Brazen Altar, which was the place of sacrifice. After the Brazen Altar, there was a Brazen Laver. After the Brazen Laver, you then entered the Holy Place. Every level is accessed by a door, but that door is opened by a key. Consider the Cosmological Order of the Kingdom.

Cosmological Order of the Kingdom
Every world is made up of kingdoms.
Every kingdom is divided into realms.
Every realm is made up of dimensions.
Every dimension is made up of levels.
Every level is accessed by doors.
Every door is opened by keys.

That key is what you call your gift. Proverbs 18:16 says, "A man's gift maketh room for him, and bringeth him before great men." So, every level is accessed by a gift! The final stage of every level is the place of reflection. Elisha had to follow Elijah through good times and difficult times; this was his ascension from the Outer Courts to the Most Holy Place. You can't get what's on the other side of that reflection unless you're willing to give up your plans, your dreams and anything that stands in the way of your calling. This is called sacrifice. Consider this—after the High Priest killed everything he needed to kill, he would then go to the Brazen Laver, look at his reflection in the water. He'd see a bloody reflection of himself. Again, the Brazen Laver had been made from the looking glasses (mirrors) of the women of Israel. In this, they had to sacrifice their vanity and how they saw themselves. In this, they had to sacrifice their reflections so that they could reflect the very nature of God (holiness). And now, there the priest stood, hovering in front of his reflection with bloody hands and feet, and with blood on his face that had splattered while he was making the sacrificial offerings. The blood reminded him of the sacrifice he'd made on behalf of the people. The blood reminded him of his own mortality. The blood reminded him of the innocent animals who had to give their lives because of Israel's sins. The blood also reminded him of the love and the grace that God had for His people. The priest would then wash himself with the water from the Brazen Laver. In the water, he could still see his reflection, but once he put his hands in it, the water became troubled and bloody. It was no longer still, and this altered his reflection. And he didn't stand there and wait for the water to settle. He went into the Holy Place, and by the time he exited it, he had to stop and wash his hands and feet again. By this time, the water was still again. At this time, he was able to see his reflection again, but it didn't look the same since the water was now bloody. Again, he had to trouble the waters with his hands and feet, making it nearly impossible for him to see a clear image of himself. And after this, he walked away. Let's review James 1:22-25 again. It reads, "But be ye doers of the word, and not hearers only, deceiving your own selves. For if any be a hearer of the word, and not a doer, he is like unto a man beholding his natural face in a glass: For he beholdeth himself, and goeth his way, and straightway forgetteth what manner of man he was. But whoso looketh into the perfect law of liberty, and continueth therein, he being not a forgetful hearer, but a doer of the work, this man shall be blessed in his deed." In other words, we'd be remiss to think that a man could stand in front of a mirror and then forget what he looks like once he walks away. We can easily identify our own reflections. The priests could readily identify their own sins, after all, before they attempted to remove the mote or the speck from Israel's eyes, they first had to examine themselves. In short, your ability to lead is represented by your ability to see. Consider what Jesus said in Matthew 15:14. "Let them alone: they be blind leaders of the blind. And if the blind lead the blind, both shall fall into the ditch." This is the ultimate Law of Reflection. In short, it states:

> **Where there is no reflection, there is no light, and where there is no light, there is no vision.**

Proverbs 29:18: Where there is no vision, the people perish: but he that keepeth the law, happy is he.

The Benefits of Reflection

Just like meditation, reflection has its benefits. But of course, what you reflect on and how you reflect on it will determine the conclusion you come to. The obvious question is, how do we use reflection when reading and reviewing the Word of God? First and foremost, remember that meditation takes a word from your mind to your heart, but reflection takes a word from your heart to your mind. For example, the majority of us are familiar with Psalm 23:1. In this verse of scripture, David said, "The LORD is my shepherd; I shall not want." If you've meditated on this scripture in the past, chances are, it's already in your heart, meaning, if I started with, "The Lord is my Shepherd," you'd follow up and finish the statement. Using the tool of reflection, what you're doing (in a sense) is regurgitating this scripture. You're bringing it back from your heart to your mind to reflect on it. And in reflection, you aren't just saying the lines, but you are looking deeper into the Word. This helps you to extract more revelation from what you've already read. But first, what exactly is revelation?

Revelation (Etymology)

c. 1300, "disclosure of information to man by a divine or supernatural agency," from Old French revelacion and directly from Latin revelationem (nominative revelatio), noun of action from past participle stem of revelare "unveil, uncover, lay bare" (see reveal). General meaning "disclosure of facts" is attested from late 14c.; meaning "striking disclosure" is from 1862. As the name of the last book of the New Testament (Revelation of St. John), it is first attested late 14c. (see apocalypse); as simply Revelations, it is first recorded 1690s.

Source: Online Etymology Dictionary

The Greek word for "revelation" is "apokalupsis," from which we get the word "apocalypse," which means "an unveiling, uncovering, revealing, revelation." Of course, the Bible starts with the book of Genesis, which is a Greek word translated to mean "origin, birth." This is where we get the words "gene, genetics and genealogy." So, in short, the word "genesis" means "the beginning" and "revelation" means "the end." But the word "end" isn't like the end of a movie! Hear me—anytime you've reached the end of a thing, you've reached the beginning of something else! Anytime you reach the end of one side of God, you have reached the beginning of another facet of Him, meaning, He is the End, but He is without ends; He is infinite. His potential is without lanes or depths or limitations! Nevertheless, the book of Revelation marks the end of the world as we know it, but the beginning of a new Heaven and a new Earth; this represents the establishment of God's system in every dimension of the high place (Heaven) and the low place (Earth). This is when all that had been hidden from us (because of our sin nature) will be revealed to us. This is when God takes away the sun so that the Son can be our Light; this is when darkness will be put in its place and Satan, his angels and everyone whose name is not found in the Book of Life will be cast into utter darkness, where the Bible says there is weeping and gnashing of teeth! Again, revelation is the revealing of a truth; it is the end of a mystery, the answer to a riddle or the missing puzzle piece that allows us to see the full picture.

But what are the benefits of reflection? After all, a lot of people are meditating and reflecting these days; many of them are involved in occultism, some are doing it for medical reasons, and then, there is Christian meditation and reflection which, of course, a lot of believers haven't yet enjoyed the benefits of. Again, this is largely because the New Age movement is claiming meditation and reflection as their own, and the church has a habit of distancing herself from anything that occultists put their hearts, hands and minds to, especially if it gains momentum. Below, you'll find six benefits of reflection.

#	Benefits	Description
1	**Strategic Thinking**	When we reflect on our choices, habits, strengths, weaknesses, and goals, this encourages us to be more strategic and less emotional when making life decisions. Reflection allows us to see patterns, strongholds and systems that have to be dismantled; this allows us to create new habits and systems that we can benefit from. Every good general in battle has to be able to think and plan strategically if he or she is going to overcome the enemy!
2	**Better Organizational**	Being emotional is the same as being unstable. And while reflection allows us to become more strategic, it does this by helping us to put

#	Benefits	Description
	Skills	things (and people) in their right or rightful places. Reflection helps us to realize what's out of place in our lives so that we can build systems and structures to facilitate change in our lives.
3	**Accountability**	One of the most effective weapons of the kingdom of darkness is victimhood. This stronghold of the mind convinces believers that they are victims, and as such, should be compensated for their troubles. This mindset encourages unforgiveness, blame and entitlement, but the antidote to this is accountability. Reflection helps us to find the common denominator (ourselves) in all of our problems. This allows us to grow, heal faster and make better choices.
4	**Increases Self Awareness**	Self-awareness makes us more cognizant of our strengths, weaknesses and limitations. Reflection allows us to take a closer look at ourselves; this way, we can strengthen those areas that are weak and set better boundaries.
5	**Improve Critical Thinking**	According to CriticalThinking.org, critical thinking is, "Critical thinking is the intellectually disciplined process of actively and skillfully conceptualizing, applying, analyzing, synthesizing, and/or evaluating information gathered from, or generated by, observation, experience, reflection, reasoning, or communication, as a guide to belief and action."
6	**Builds Faith**	Faith is the substance of things hoped for and the evidence of things not seen. Reflection helps us to remember, not just what we've gone through, but the God who brought us out, along with how He brought us out. When the Israelites came out of Egypt, God encouraged them to remember what He'd brought them through. This is because whenever they went through a dark space, He wanted them to remember that He was and is in control.

Of course, there are more benefits to reflecting, but the point is—your mind is a wide and expansive space; it is like a wilderness. It is without limitations, ends or edges. In it, there are all types of issues that arise. Your goal is to grow what you want to keep and uproot what you want to get rid of. Reflection helps you to see this space with more precision; this way, you can be more intentional with your growth and deliverance.

Meditation Moment

The LORD reigneth; let the earth rejoice; let the multitude of isles be glad thereof. Clouds and darkness are round about him: righteousness and judgment are the habitation of his throne. A fire goeth before him, and burneth up his enemies round about. His lightnings enlightened the world: the earth saw, and trembled. The hills melted like wax at the presence of the LORD, at the presence of the Lord of the whole earth. The heavens declare his righteousness, and all the people see his glory. Confounded be all they that serve graven images, that boast themselves of idols: worship him, all ye gods. Zion heard, and was glad; and the daughters of Judah rejoiced because of thy judgments, O LORD. For thou, LORD, art high above all the earth: thou art exalted far above all gods. Ye that love the LORD, hate evil: he preserveth the souls of his saints; he delivereth them out of the hand of the wicked. Light is sown for the righteous, and gladness for the upright in heart. Rejoice in the LORD, ye righteous; and give thanks at the remembrance of his holiness.

What are the meditation points for you? List them below.

Meditation Points	
1	
2	
3	
4	
5	
6	
7	
8	
9	
10	
11	
12	
13	

WORD STUDY

List the words that stand out to you and conduct a word study.
Again, if you don't have space in this document, use another document.

Word	
Definition or Etymology	

Word	
Definition or Etymology	

Word	
Definition or Etymology	

LET'S REFLECT!

What did you learn from the previous chapter?
How do you plan to apply this knowledge to your life?

_____

_____

_____

_____

_____

_____

_____

_____

_____

_____

_____

_____

_____

MY ALARM CLOCK

Did You Know?
Research shows that creative people sleep more than non-creative people, but they don't sleep as well.

Did You Know?
Oneirophobia is the fear of nightmares or dreams.

Did You Know?
Sleep deprivation increases the risk of cancer.

Did You Know?
Seventy-five percent of people who suffer from depression also suffer from sleep deprivation.

Did You Know?
Meditation helps to take your mind off of distracting thoughts, thus, allowing you to fall asleep faster!

Using the boxes below, record the dates when you had trouble sleeping.
Did you meditate that night? Write yes or no in the box provided.

Monday	Tuesday	Wednesday	Thursday	Friday	Saturday	Sunday

BREATHE

Breathe (Etymology)
"to draw air into and expel it from the lungs; to inhale and exhale (a scent, etc.)," c. 1200, not in Old English, but it retains the original Old English vowel of its source word, breath. To breathe (one's) last "die" is from 1590s. To breathe down the back of (someone's) neck "be close behind" is by 1946. Related: Breathed; breathing.
Source: Online Etymology Dictionary

Breathe
Psuché (Greek)
(a) the vital breath, breath of life, (b) the human soul, (c) the soul as the seat of affections and will, (d) the self, (e) a human person, an individual.
Source: Strong's Concordance

The Kundalini Spirit
Kundalini
: the yogic life force that is held to lie coiled at the base of the spine until it is aroused and sent to the head to trigger enlightenment.
Source: Merriam Webster

Satan has tried to recreate or mimic everything that God created and all of what God stands for. The goal of this is to create confusion so that he can deceive people into believing that he is on an equal plane with God, when he's not. How can the created thing be equal to or greater than the Creator? It's simply impossible. Nevertheless, this is the deception that the world is feeding on, after all, there are people who think they are greater than or equally matched with God, and there are people who think that Satan is on the same spectrum as God, when neither of these are true. But it does mean that Satan has successfully deceived the world, and the new fruit that they're biting into is that they don't need YAHWEH. Consider Eve's deception. Satan told her that she could be "as gods, knowing good and evil" if only she would disobey God and eat from the Tree of the Knowledge of Good and Evil. In other words, he made her the same offer that he'd made God's angels when he'd led them into the darkness to seduce them. And like the third of the angels who fell into this snare, Eve found herself experiencing something she'd never experienced before—temptation! Please note that the Greek word for "temptation" is "peirasmos" and it literally means "an experiment." Let's briefly look at a few scriptures.

Genesis 1:24-25	And God said, Let the earth bring forth the living creature after his kind, cattle, and creeping thing, and beast of the earth after his kind: and it was so. And God made the beast of the earth after his kind, and cattle after their kind, and every thing that creepeth upon the earth after his kind: and God saw that it was good.
Genesis 3:1	Now the serpent was more subtil than any beast of the field which the LORD God had made. And he said unto the woman, Yea, hath God said, Ye shall not eat of every tree of the garden?
Genesis 3:14-15	And the LORD God said unto the serpent, Because thou hast done this, thou art cursed above all cattle, and above every beast of the field; upon thy belly shalt thou go, and dust shalt thou eat all the days of thy life: And I will put enmity between thee and the woman, and between thy seed and her seed; it shall bruise thy head, and thou shalt bruise his heel.

Notice that God created every living creature after its own kind; this included the serpent. But according to Genesis 3, the serpent was subtil, meaning it was cunning, crafty, or tricky. As we browse the scriptures a little more, we see God punishing the serpent by casting it onto its belly, meaning, He removed its ability to walk upright. In other words, He cut its legs from under it. But hear me—the snake and Satan were two separate entities working together as a unit, which is why God punished them as a unit.

The Hebrew word for "snake" is also associated with the word "divination." The Greek word for "divination" ironically enough is "puthón," from which we get the word "python." On that infamous day in the Garden, Satan bewitched Eve. Now, this doesn't mean that she was possessed and couldn't think for herself. It simply means that the minute Satan started talking to her, he was slowly bringing her under the influence of a lie. The more she listened, the more she could feel her senses beginning to awaken. Before long, she found herself so immersed in the lie that she was willing to risk it all just to experiment with Satan's words. Understand this—the goal of an experiment is to prove or disprove something. The minute Eve started doubting or questioning God, her perspective of Him changed, even though He was and is still the same. Just like Lucifer's pipes began to bend and twist whenever he would steal away to meditate on the imaginations of his wicked heart, Eve's mind began to twist and contort until she gave into temptation. This was divination in practice. Hear me—to be under the influence doesn't mean that you are unaware of what you're doing. It simply means that something is affecting your natural cognitive functions.

What exactly did Satan offer Eve? In short, he told her that he could awaken a "third eye." Remember, when God cast the serpent onto its belly, it had legs. A snake with legs would look a lot like a lizard, don't you think? Amazingly enough, many types of lizards have a third eye called a parietal or pineal eye located at the top of their skulls. And while this eye doesn't form images, it can detect light. Its sole purpose is hormone production and reproduction, even though it is attached to both retinas. Scientists believe that this was once an eye that actually functioned, but over the years because of evolution, it lost most of its functionality. Of course, this is just a theory. Let's look at what WikiVet had to say about this organ.

Parietal Eye
This sensory organ is connected to the central nervous system and the pineal gland by the small parietal nerve. It functions in hormone production (including reproduction) and thermoregulation (by acting as a light dosimeter). It detects both UV light and heat. Although sensitive to changes in light, it cannot form images. By detecting light and dark it allows lizards to detect the movement of predators. Sometimes referred to as "pineal eye" or "third eye", it visible as an opalescent gray spot on the top of some lizard's heads.
Source: WikiVet/Lizard Eye

The point is, the serpent was once a lizard-like creature who could have potentially had a third eye, but before it fell, it is possible that this was a fully functioning eye. Ironically enough, many occultists speak nonstop about opening what they call a "third eye." In other words, people are still chasing after false knowledge, false light (revelation) and lies in hopes that they too will get in tune with their "higher selves" without having to go the God-route to get it. Consider 2 Corinthians 11:4 (ESV), which reads, "And no wonder, for even Satan disguises himself as an angel of light." In short, Satan does disguise himself as an angel of God and an angel of revelation, so this "white light" that occultists and New Age followers teach about is not the light or revelation of God. It is false light. It is Satan disguising himself so that he can promote his doctrine to the masses, and anyone who opens himself or herself up to this "energy" as they call it, subjects or submits himself or herself to a demonic entity commonly known as the Kundalini spirit.

First off, what or who is Kundalini? It is one of the many spirits that got cast out of Heaven. Please understand that before Lucifer and his angels decided to betray God, they were good spirits, but after they attempted to establish their own kingdom, they took on new roles.

Kundalini

Kundalini (Sanskrit: कुण्डलिनी *kuṇḍalinī*, pronunciation, "coiled snake"), in Hinduism is a form of divine feminine energy (or *shakti*) believed to be located at the base of the spine, in the *muladhara*. It is an important concept in Śhaiva Tantra, where it is believed to be a force or power associated with the divine feminine or the formless aspect of the Goddess. This energy in the body, when cultivated and awakened through tantric practice, is believed to lead to spiritual liberation. Kuṇḍalinī is associated with Parvati or Adi Parashakti, the supreme being in Shaktism; and with the goddesses Bhairavi and Kubjika. The term, along with practices associated with it, was adopted into Hatha yoga in the 9th century. It has since then been adopted into other forms of Hinduism as well as modern spirituality and New age thought.

Kuṇḍalinī awakenings have been described as occurring by means of a variety of methods. Many systems of yoga focus on awakening Kuṇḍalinī through meditation; pranayama breathing; the practice of asana and chanting of mantras. Kundalini Yoga is influenced by Shaktism and Tantra schools of Hinduism. It derives its name from its focus upon the awakening of kundalini energy through regular practice of Mantra, Tantra, Yantra, Asanas or Meditation. The Kuṇḍalinī experience is frequently reported to be a distinct feeling of electric current running along the spine.

Source: WikiVet/Lizard Eye

In layman's terms, Kundalini is a demonic spirit (devil) that associates itself with some forms of yoga, meditation and other pagan practices. Again, yoga within itself is not demonic, but it does have pagan origins. Meditation is good when its used as a tool to study the Word of God, but anytime man takes a practice that God created and removes God from it, that practice becomes perverted. So yes, trying to awaken Kundalini is a demonic practice that can and does end with people unknowingly embracing dark spirits. Also commonly known as the Python spirit, Kundalini is often known to mimic or impersonate the Holy Spirit. Remember:

1. You are a spirit.
2. You possess a soul.
3. You live in a body.

The goal of any and every demonic entity is:

1. To kill.
2. To steal.
3. To destroy.

But the enemy will always promise you opposite of what he intends to give you, after all, he is a fallen angel, and he is a liar. As a matter of fact, the Bible calls him the father of all lies. And as such, his goal is to get you under his influence in the same manner in which he deceived a third of God's angels, and in the same manner in which he deceived Eve. He still masquerades as an angel of light, and unfortunately, many believers and unbelievers alike are unknowingly embracing him by seeking after light, energy, vibrations, and spiritual things outside of God.

- **Light:** God is Light (see 1 John 1:5), and any other spiritual light is false, generic, and demonic.
- **Energy:** God is all-powerful. Any and every other power is subject to Him. Any other spiritual power outside of Him is illegal and demonic.
- **Vibrations:** God is Love. Love moves. When God speaks, everything moves. Where God is, you will find life, and wherever you find life, you will find movement. In other words, there are no energy fields (auras) around people; there's simply life in people. A negative person doesn't release negative energy; it simply doesn't exist. We are simply sensitive to the moods of everyone else around us BECAUSE WE ARE ALL CONNECTED through a common source: Adam. The more intimate or connected we are, the more sensitive we'll be to the moods of the people around us.

Again, many people are turning to false gods and false doctrines in an attempt to find themselves. God warned us that this would happen in 1 Timothy 4:1-2, which reads, "Now the Spirit speaketh expressly, that in the latter times some shall depart from the faith, giving heed to seducing spirits, and doctrines of devils; speaking lies in hypocrisy; having their conscience seared with a hot iron." Occultists and New Age proponents simply capitalize off of two sources:

1. **The Bible:** Just like any side-street hustler, many of the people who standardize, promote or even create demonic doctrines take their beliefs from the Bible itself, but because they hate God or because they are angry with God and don't want to give Him glory or credit, they simply rebrand what they read using scientific words. From there, they repackage and resell it to the unsuspecting and the hungry.
2. **Science:** Science is not an enemy of the faith! True science points to God, but many scientists who are against God will never publish evidence that supports His existence. So, they intentionally manipulate the evidence to point away from Him; that is, until a true scientist comes and disproves their arguments or their theories. Howbeit, many of the top gurus in the New Age movement take what scientists discover and repackage it as spiritual knowledge.

The Kundalini (Python) spirit is, in short, a spirit of divination or witchcraft. We see this spirit in operation in Acts 16:16-18, which reads, "And it came to pass, as we went to prayer, a certain damsel possessed with a spirit of divination met us, which brought her masters much gain by soothsaying: The same followed Paul and us, and cried, saying, These men are the servants of the most high God, which shew unto us the way of salvation. And this did she many days. But Paul, being grieved, turned and said to the spirit, I command thee in the name of Jesus Christ to come out of her. And he came out the same hour." You'll notice that it tried to infiltrate a move of God by speaking truths and using flattery. Nevertheless, the Apostle Paul knew that this spirit was not from God because:

1. It interrupted or began to speak whenever they went into prayer.
2. The slave girl gave glory to the men, and not to the Most High God. This is called flattery, and it is a common demonic practice designed to allow a person to gain access to a particular person, group, movement or organization.
3. She was a soothsayer, and she used her "abilities" to make money for her masters. In other words, you can't be both a psychic and a prophet; you can't serve two gods or two contrary kingdoms!
4. The woman followed the men for several days. What this means is that the woman herself wanted to be free; this is why the deliverance was effective. Python seized every moment that she was in their presence to disguise itself with hopes that it could infiltrate their camp, but the woman herself wanted to be set free. She was like the woman with the issue of blood, but she didn't touch the men's garments, nor did she crawl after them. Instead, she pursued them until Paul could no longer deny that tug he felt on his spirit; he could feel the virtue or anointing of God rising up in him. From there, he became grieved (he burned with compassion), and he did what he was called to do. He put Satan and his powers in their place!

The chart below lists some characteristics or traits of the Kundalini (Python) spirit.

Feeling Trapped, Constricted	Chronic Procrastination	Isolation/Distrust of People
Weariness	Lack of Ambition	Depression
Lethargy	Poverty	Suicidal Thoughts/Tendencies
Apathy	Indifference	Hopelessness
Sabotage	Trouble Staying Focused	Confusion
Inability to Pray	Trouble Reading the Bible	Inability to Worship

Of course, this is not an extensive or an expansive list on the characteristics of this particular spirit, but these are some of the major complications or symptoms of Python. Below, I have answered three of the most common questions people tend to ask when they hear about this particular spirit.

Can I pick up the Python spirit if I have unknowingly gotten involved in New Age or occultist practices?

Yes and no. No, you won't pick up a demon just because you've meditated, for example, using one of the postures used by Hindus to worship their many gods. However, the devil is progressive, so it could start off with you using one of the postures, and then you may find yourself gradually embracing more Hindu practices, and finally, their beliefs. In your progression, you may find yourself buying statues used to represent Hindu gods and placing them all throughout your home. Next, you may find yourself using some of their quotes. From there, you may graduate to watching videos that promote their beliefs, and finally, you may find yourself trying to integrate or marry their beliefs to the Christian faith. This is called double-mindedness. The best practice to guard your heart is through education and information. Don't do anything that you haven't researched, especially if it borders a belief system that's contrary to your faith. Be accountable; talk with your pastor and ask questions.

A lot of New Age beliefs seem to be sound and they even border what the Bible teaches. How do you explain this?

First and foremost, remember that Satan does disguise himself as an angel of light. What this means is that Satan doesn't just come out and tell a blatant, outright lie! He gives you truths seasoned with questions, and if one or more of those questions is effective in dislodging what you believe about God, he then offers you a lie. Consider what he did with Eve. He asked her, "Did God really say, 'You can't eat from any tree in the garden'?" The question within itself was loaded. It was designed to dislodge or cause Eve to question whether she'd heard God the correct way. Hear me—the first level of warfare is when you begin to question whether you heard God. What occultists and other false faiths do, especially New Agers, is they take scientific and medical information that has already been established as facts, and they repackage it as religion. They even do this with scriptures. As I mentioned earlier, they'll take, for example, Galatians 6:7, which reads, "Be not deceived; God is not mocked: for whatsoever a man soweth, that shall he also reap" and call it "karma." The law of sowing and reaping is absolute; in other words, it works for believers and non-believers. Remember, it rains on the just and the unjust! So by taking what God said and giving another name to it, the proponents of these faiths are able to appear (to the naked eye) to be sound when, in truth, they are not.

How do I get delivered from the Python spirit if I have somehow picked it up?

Renounce it and command it to leave! Satan can only stay where (1) he's wanted and (2) he's tolerated. If you don't want him, don't tolerate him. Also, if you're not familiar with the ministry of deliverance or if you're uncomfortable performing self-deliverance, simply speak to one of the ministers at your church and ask them if they'd lead you through deliverance. If your church hasn't embraced the ministry of deliverance, go to a deliverance conference in your area. Find sound, biblical leaders who are known for ministering deliverance, and look at their itineraries to see if and when they'll be in your area. If you're hungry or desperate enough, consider traveling to one of their conferences if they are outside of your area. Lastly, there are some people who administer virtual deliverance (over the phone or via Skype). Just ask the Lord to lead you to the right person or the right people. Below, you'll find a renunciation that you can do to free yourself from its grip or, at minimum, jump-start the process.

Step One

Study and meditate on scriptures about deliverance.

Step Two

Spend time in prayer and in worship.

Step Thee

Repent for your sins, the sins of your parents and the sins of your ancestors. Renounce their wicked ways, for example, say, "I repent for and renounce the witchcraft in my bloodline in Jesus name."

Step Four

Ask the Lord to set you free. Remind Him of His Word (Luke 10:19).

Step Five

Command Satan and his accomplices to leave you now in Jesus name!
Note: See renunciation below.

Step Six

Receive your deliverance! Exhale after every renunciation.

Step Seven

Ask the Lord to give you a fresh in-filling of His Holy Spirit.

Renunciation

I repent for my sins, the sins of my parents and the sins of my ancestors, both known and unknown. I bind the strongman and command it to leave me now in the name of Jesus
(Exhale)

I renounce every unclean spirit attached to my name and my bloodline in the name of Jesus!
(Exhale)

I renounce the spirit of divination! Python, I command you to leave me now and go to the feet of Jesus!
(Exhale)

I close every demonic access door that's open in my life, and I command those doors to shut, and I seal them shut with the blood of Christ Jesus! In Jesus name!
(Exhale)

Don't forget to ask the Lord to give you a fresh infilling of His Holy Spirit! (Inhale). And lastly, remember that one can place a thousand to flight, but two can chase ten thousand. In other words, if you need a substantial amount of deliverance, it is always a good practice to enlist someone to assist you. Jesus sent out His disciples in twos, meaning, you were never designed to do this alone!

Imagine the moment when Satan was cast out of Heaven. Consider this—the word "heave" according to Merriam Webster, means:

1. To throw, cast.
2. To utter with obvious effort or with a deep breath.
3. An act or instance of throwing: hurl.

Heave

Old English hebban "to lift, raise; lift up, exalt" (class VI strong verb; past tense hof, past participle hafen), from Proto-Germanic *hafjan (source also of Old Norse hefja, Dutch heffen, German heben, Gothic hafjan "to lift, raise"), from PIE *kap-yo-, from root *kap- "to grasp."

> The sense evolution would be "to take, take hold of," thence "lift."
> Related to have (Old English habban "to hold, possess"). Meaning "to throw" is from 1590s. Nautical meaning "haul or pull" in any direction is from 1620s. Intransitive use from early 14c. as "be raised or forced up;" 1610s as "rise and fall with alternate motion." Sense of "retch, make an effort to vomit" is first attested c. 1600. Related: Heaved; heaving. Nautical heave-ho was a chant in lifting (c. 1300, hevelow).
>
> Noun: 1570s, from heave (v.). Meaning "a dismissal" is from 1944.
>
> *Source: Online Etymology Dictionary*

In short, God created the expanse that we know as Heaven with the heave or blowing of His breath. And as in all things created by God, one blow from His nostrils, created a system.

Third Heaven	Second Heaven	First Heaven

All the same, when God cast Satan out of Heaven, He did so simply by heaving or, better yet, exhaling. This is similar to what we now do when ministering deliverance to ourselves. We command unclean spirits to come out (exit through our airways). This is because demons are spirits (breaths). This is why they are expelled through coughing, sneezing, vomiting and flatulence. So, as you renounce them, exhale. What you're doing is similar to what God did in Heaven. Note, Jesus cast them out of your spirit, and then, He gave you the power and the authority to cast them out of your soul and your body.

The Words We Breathe

How did God make man?		
First, He created his spirit.	**Next, He made his body.**	**Finally, He made his soul.**
So God created man in his own image, in the image of God created he him; male and female created he them.	And the LORD God formed man of the dust of the ground ...	And breathed into his nostrils the breath of life; and man became a living soul.
Genesis 1:27	Genesis 2:7	Genesis 2:7

Before God created bodies for Adam and Eve, He created their spirits. He did this on the sixth day of Creation. Remember, a spirit is a breath and a word of God intermingled together. You are an individualized word of God. When God spoke you into existence, He also breathed you into existence. Remember, nothing God says can ever return to Him void. This is why Heaven and Hell exists. Spirits are eternal creatures, and as such, they need to be housed in eternity. When your spirit leaves your body, you will return to God to be judged. This again is when God inhales. Similarly, whenever you speak a word, you breathe life into that word. Our words aren't just sounds that can be translated; they are spirits (not demons) that go forth to carry out whatever it is that we've spoken. This is what it means to be created in the image of God. This is also why Jesus said in Matthew 18:18, "Verily I say unto you, Whatsoever ye shall bind on earth shall be bound in heaven: and whatsoever ye shall loose on earth shall be loosed in heaven." In other words, there is power in our tongues, and whenever we use that power for evil, it is called witchcraft! How do we bind and how do we loose? With our tongues, of course! Proverbs 18:20 says it like this, "A man's belly shall be satisfied with the fruit of his mouth; and with the increase of his lips shall he be filled." Whatever we speak, we give permission to live! This is why we have to be mindful of what we say.

Before God created a body for you, He created your spirit. Consider what the Lord said to the Prophet Jeremiah in Jeremiah 1:5. "Before I formed thee in the belly I knew thee; and before thou camest forth out of the womb I sanctified thee, and I ordained thee a prophet unto the nations." Before Jeremiah was formed in the belly of his mother, before he had a body, he existed as a spirit. The same is true for you. Your parents didn't create you; God did. Your parents were just the vehicles that God used to birth your spirit in the Earth. When you were in your mother's womb, you couldn't breathe on your own. Your lungs were in development, so the umbilical cord of your mother provided you with the oxygen you needed. You couldn't speak, you couldn't breathe; the only part of you that could respond to stimuli was your body and your lungs. Using your vocal cord, whenever you experienced negative stimuli, you responded by crying. You'd do this by filling your lungs with air, and then, expelling that air. This was an instinctual response to a need that you had. As you got older, your vocabulary increased. You began to speak what you heard your parents, your siblings, your relatives, your teachers and your peers say. As always, before speaking, you would fill your lungs with air, and then, expel that air by releasing words. Some of those words were good; some of them were bad. And once you got saved, you came to understand the power of your words. One day, you realized that you were literally living in the world you'd created with your words. And if you were ever introduced to the ministry of deliverance, at some point, you found yourself canceling out many of the words you'd given life to. But maybe, you did it religiously and erroneously by saying, "I cancel those words in Jesus name!" This is because you didn't realize how legalities work. Consider the story of Esther. Let's look at a few scriptures.

Esther 3:8-12	Esther 8:3-10
And Haman said unto king Ahasuerus, There is a certain people scattered abroad and dispersed among the people in all the provinces of thy kingdom; and their laws are diverse from all people; neither keep they the king's laws: therefore it is not for the king's profit to suffer them. If it please the king, let it be written that they may be destroyed: and I will pay ten thousand talents of silver to the hands of those that have the charge of the business, to bring it into the king's treasuries. And the king took his ring from his hand, and gave it unto Haman the son of Hammedatha the Agagite, the Jews' enemy. And the king said unto Haman, The silver is given to thee, the people also, to do with them as it seemeth good to thee.	And Esther spake yet again before the king, and fell down at his feet, and besought him with tears to put away the mischief of Haman the Agagite, and his device that he had devised against the Jews. Then the king held out the golden sceptre toward Esther. So Esther arose, and stood before the king, and said, If it please the king, and if I have found favour in his sight, and the thing seem right before the king, and I be pleasing in his eyes, let it be written to reverse the letters devised by Haman the son of Hammedatha the Agagite, which he wrote to destroy the Jews which are in all the king's provinces: For how can I endure to see the evil that shall come unto my people? or how can I endure to see the destruction of my kindred?
Then were the king's scribes called on the thirteenth day of the first month, and there was written according to all that Haman had commanded unto the king's lieutenants, and to the governors that were over every province, and to the rulers of every people of every province according to the writing thereof, and to every people after their language; in the name of king Ahasuerus was it written, and sealed with the king's ring.	Then the king Ahasuerus said unto Esther the queen and to Mordecai the Jew, Behold, I have given Esther the house of Haman, and him they have hanged upon the gallows, because he laid his hand upon the Jews. Write ye also for the Jews, as it liketh you, in the king's name, and seal it with the king's ring: for the writing which is written in the king's name, and sealed with the king's ring, may no man reverse.
	Then were the king's scribes called at that time in the third month, that is, the month Sivan, on the three and twentieth day thereof; and it was written according to all that Mordecai commanded unto the Jews, and to the lieutenants, and the deputies and rulers of the provinces which are from India unto

Esther 3:8-12	Esther 8:3-10
	Ethiopia, an hundred twenty and seven provinces, unto every province according to the writing thereof, and unto every people after their language, and to the Jews according to their writing, and according to their language. And he wrote in the king Ahasuerus' name, and sealed it with the king's ring, and sent letters by posts on horseback, and riders on mules, camels, and young dromedaries.

Hear me—anytime a king gave an edict or decree, even the king himself could not cancel it out! It was legal and could not be retracted! King Ahasuerus could not go against the words he'd spoken. He couldn't send out letters that said, "The former decree is canceled! Don't lay a finger on the Jews!" No, he had to create another decree, one that gave the Jews the power and the right to fight back! This is similar to how God does a thing! He is bound by His words; whatever God speaks, He can't take back (it is impossible for Him to tell a lie), but He can create another Word to counter it! Get it?! Jesus is the living Word of God! He countered the Old Testament, so while all scriptures are God-breathed and beneficial for teaching, for reproof, correction and instruction, we are no longer under the curse of the Law. Unbelievers, however, are under the curse of the Law because God's Word cannot and will never return to Him void. Jesus came and redeemed us from the curse of the Law; He is not only the Word made flesh, but He also fulfilled the first Messianic prophecy ever spoken. In Genesis 3:15, we find YAHWEH speaking to Satan. He says, "And I will put enmity between you and the woman, and between your seed and her Seed; He shall bruise your head, and you shall bruise His heel." Who is the He referred to in this scripture? Jesus Christ, of course! And Satan bruised His heels on the cross, but Jesus bruised his head (authority)! Again, in order for King Ahasuerus to prevent the slaughter of the Jews, he had to issue another edict! In order for God to stop the Old Testament Law from condemning you to an eternity of separation from Him, He had to issue another edict: Jesus Christ! The same is true for you! You can't cancel words by saying, "I cancel those words!" No! You have to speak a higher word. For example, if I found myself in depression and I started speaking death over myself, I can't just turn around and say, "I cancel those words," because both statements are on an equal plane. It only creates an environment for double-mindedness to formulate and eventually become normalized in my life. No, I could either speak the Word of God over myself since it is a "higher" word or I can say what David said, "I will live and not die! I will live and declare the works of the Lord!" But I can't just leave it at that; I'd follow it up with, "In Jesus name!" (Additionally, I must make sure what I decree over myself is in alignment with what God said about me.) What I am doing is sealing that statement with the blood of Jesus! Remember, everything that King Ahasuerus wrote as an edict, he sealed it with wax. Everything God said, He sealed it with blood! And anything we want to legalize and place over another edict or word, we need to apply the blood of Jesus to! Again, this is because words aren't just spoken, they are breathed.

Why is this important? Because in the practice of meditation, you aren't just sitting in silence, there are times when you need to speak. This is a great time to reflect on some of the things you've said and to counter those words with the Word of God. Hear me—you don't have to be religious with it! You don't have to remember every word curse you've spoken over yourself! You simply need to speak the Word of God over yourself, and if you happen to remember any evil you've spoken over yourself or someone else, your job is to cancel it out, after all, you shall have whatsoever you say. Yes, this includes the words you've spoken over others. As you breathe in and breathe out, speak God's Word over yourself. Before you start your meditation, write down a few scriptures to meditate on and speak over yourself. If you've been dealing with depression, for example, you can use the following scriptures:

Psalm 9:9	The LORD also will be a refuge for the oppressed, a refuge in times of trouble.
Psalm 34:17	The righteous cry, and the LORD heareth, and delivereth them out of all their troubles.
Isaiah 40:29-31	He giveth power to the faint; and to them that have no might he increaseth strength. Even the youths shall faint and be weary, and the young men shall utterly fall: But they that wait upon the LORD shall renew their strength; they shall mount up with wings as eagles; they shall run, and not be weary; and they shall walk, and not faint.
1 Peter 5:7	Casting all your care upon him; for he careth for you.
Isaiah 41:10	Fear thou not; for I am with thee: be not dismayed; for I am thy God: I will strengthen thee; yea, I will help thee; yea, I will uphold thee with the right hand of my righteousness.

The point is—meditation isn't just about sitting in a quiet space and trying to calm your mind, it is also about changing the way that your mind operates. This is done one word at a time since the fuel of the mind are words. Think of it this way—you are surrounded by words every single day of your life. When you go to work, you are surrounded by words; when you come home, you are surrounded by words; when you go to church, you are surrounded by words. Research suggests that the average person hears no less than 20,000-30,0000 words a day. The average woman, according to research, speaks around 17,000-20,000 words in a single day. The average man, on the other hand, speaks around 7,000 words a day. You don't just live in a world of words, you are a word. Now, do you understand why the quote, "Sticks and stones may break my bones, but words will never hurt me" is nothing but a poetic lie? Words do hurt because you are a word! So, when you sit down (or stand) to meditate, your goal is to focus on:

1. What God said about you (the Word of God).
2. What you think about yourself.

You should center your focus around making your words about you (and others) line up with God's Word about you (and others). The art of meditation may have been hijacked by the New Age movement, and the goal of non-Christian meditation is about stilling and calming the mind, but hear me—this is a temporary fix to a life-long problem. Meditation is a Christian concept that should always involve God because He is our center, our core and our focus. Outside of Him and His Word, meditation is pretty much creating a pocket or a space for you to escape the world of words that you live in, and while this may serve as a temporary refuge, it has no power to cancel out the words that have formed your world. The Word of God is powerful enough to create a whole new world for you; one where every other contrary word has no power, authority or permission to exist; in other words, they have no choice but to fall to the ground!

Man Versus Mankind

The respiratory system is made up of ten parts. They are:

Nose & Nasal Cavity	Mouth	Throat (Pharynx)	Voice Box (Larynx)
Bronchi (Airways)	Sinuses	Windpipe (Trachea)	Lungs
Diaphragm	Bronchioles	Air Sacs (Alveoli)	Capillaries

In order for us to breathe, all of these parts must be open and active, meaning, they can't be inflamed or swollen. But for the sake of this presentation, we are only going to focus on the major organs in this system; they are:

- Nose
- Mouth
- Throat

- Voice Box
- Windpipe
- Lungs
- Diaphragm

Nose

Nose, the prominent structure between the eyes that serves as the entrance to the respiratory tract and contains the olfactory organ. It provides air for respiration, serves the sense of smell, conditions the air by filtering, warming, and moistening it, and cleans itself of foreign debris extracted from inhalations.

Source: Encyclopedia Britannica

Mouth

Mouth, also called **oral cavity** or **buccal cavity**, in human anatomy, orifice through which food and air enter the body. The mouth opens to the outside at the lips and empties into the throat at the rear; its boundaries are defined by the lips, cheeks, hard and soft palates, and glottis. It is divided into two sections: the vestibule, the area between the cheeks and the teeth, and the oral cavity proper. The latter section is mostly filled by the tongue, a large muscle firmly anchored to the floor of the mouth by the frenulum linguae. In addition to its primary role in the intake and initial digestion of food, the mouth and its structures are essential in humans to the formation of speech.

Source: Encyclopedia Britannica

Throat

Pharynx, (Greek: "throat") cone-shaped passageway leading from the oral and nasal cavities in the head to the esophagus and larynx. The pharynx chamber serves both respiratory and digestive functions. Thick fibres of muscle and connective tissue attach the pharynx to the base of the skull and surrounding structures. Both circular and longitudinal muscles occur in the walls of the pharynx; the circular muscles form constrictions that help push food to the esophagus and prevent air from being swallowed, while the longitudinal fibres lift the walls of the pharynx during swallowing.

Source: Encyclopedia Britannica

Voice Box

Larynx, also called **voice box**, a hollow, tubular structure connected to the top of the windpipe (trachea); air passes through the larynx on its way to the lungs. The larynx also produces vocal sounds and prevents the passage of food and other foreign particles into the lower respiratory tracts.

Source: Encyclopedia Britannica

Lungs

Lung, in air-breathing vertebrates, either of the two large organs of respiration located in the chest cavity and responsible for adding oxygen to and removing carbon dioxide from the blood. In humans each lung is encased in a thin membranous sac called the pleura, and each is connected with the trachea (windpipe) by its main bronchus (large air passageway) and with the heart by the pulmonary arteries. The lungs are soft, light, spongy, elastic organs that normally, after birth, always contain some air. If healthy, they will float in water and crackle when squeezed; diseased lungs sink.

Source: Encyclopedia Britannica

Diaphragm

Diaphragm, dome-shaped, muscular and membranous structure that separates the thoracic (chest) and abdominal cavities in mammals; it is the principal muscle of respiration.
The muscles of the diaphragm arise from the lower part of the sternum (breastbone), the lower six ribs, and the lumbar (loin) vertebrae of the spine and are attached to a central membranous tendon. Contraction of the diaphragm increases the internal height of the thoracic cavity, thus lowering its internal pressure and causing inspiration of air. Relaxation of the diaphragm and the natural elasticity of lung tissue and the thoracic cage produce expiration. The diaphragm is also important in expulsive actions—e.g., coughing, sneezing, vomiting, crying, and expelling feces, urine, and, in parturition, the fetus. The diaphragm is pierced by many structures, notably the esophagus, aorta, and inferior vena cava, and is occasionally subject to herniation (rupture). Small holes in the membranous portion of the diaphragm sometimes allow abnormal accumulations of fluid or air to move from the abdominal cavity (where pressure is positive during inspiration) into the pleural spaces of the chest (where pressure is negative during inspiration). Spasmodic inspiratory movement of the diaphragm produces the characteristic sound known as hiccupping.

Source: Encyclopedia Britannica

The reason I wanted to list all of these organs is because I want you to see the complexity of, not just the respiratory system, but a system as a whole. When God breathed life into Adam, Adam became a living soul—we understand this, but what most people haven't fully grasped is how much detail went into forming the man! Of course, we could argue about the climate in the Garden of Eden and whether or not man's system was as complex as it is today. I could suggest and maybe even prove to you that the system of man (God's original design) and mankind (fallen man) are not the same because our new and revised system had to be equipped with the ability to flush out, cast out and filter out pollutants (waste), none of which were found in the Garden of Eden. It is possible that all the couple had to do was inhale; that is, take in all that God had done and created, and exhale; that is to reproduce what God had done. Everything in the Garden was pure, good, and free of the poisons produced by sin, so there was no need for the couple's body to filter out any waste. It is possible that they didn't have to expel any waste since their bodies would have potentially used everything they'd eaten for fuel. Nevertheless, they fell, and man's system had to be updated (not upgraded). So now, we inhale oxygen, but we exhale carbon dioxide and other gases. This is all a part of another system. In this system, we provide the fuel (carbon dioxide) needed for the plants on our Earth to grow. Those plants, in return, provide us with oxygen. You'll notice that everything that God created is a part of a system, and every part of a system, both small and great, is necessary for the functionality of that system. The same is true for the system of the soul which, of course, we know is directly connected to our breathing. Again, let's look at the setup of man's body and his soul to get a better understanding.

Mankind	Spirit	Soul	Body
Soul	Mind	Will	Emotions

Remember, the mind is broken down into three parts; they are:

Levels of the Mind	Conscious	Subconscious	Unconscious

As you can see, man is a complex system within himself, and every part or dimension of mankind has its own unique system, all of which are centered around allowing the man to live (breathe) and think (function). But sin makes this difficult; it clouds our minds, perverts our will and hijacks our emotions. In other words, it bends us in the same manner in which it bent Lucifer's pipes. He was God's Light-Bearer, meaning, he was designed to function in the light or the revelation of God. The revelation of God is found in the presence of God. The presence of God is found in the will of God, and the will of God is found in the Word of God. Lucifer saw the darkness, and like a man in search of real estate, he walked into the darkness and surveyed it. But in the darkness, his system began to malfunction; in the darkness, his light began to dim. Slowly but surely, he started morphing into a hideous creature; in other words, he no longer looked like the God he had been designed to represent. His body was a complex and beautiful system comprised of precious jewels and instruments. His entrails (instruments) were connected to his mouth, so whenever God spoke through him, the sound would pierce through his body. Whenever the angels would worship God, the sounds of their worship would also penetrate his body and come out as one beautiful sound to the Lord. But when he decided to keep the praise for himself, he became constipated. He tried to steal God's glory, but it was too much for his body to bear. So, in the darkness, his body began to twist and contort so much so that whenever he tried to praise God again, he didn't sound the same. He sounded like someone whose lungs had been severely inflamed. And when he was cast out of Heaven, he could no longer be God's Light-Bearer, so his system had to change to adapt to his new role and his new environment. His beauty became a thing of the past. His once beautiful voice was but a distant memory, and the angels that he'd deceived went from being creatures of praise to complainers. In other words, their systems changed as well. Again, the same is true for mankind. Our systems had to change to adapt to the world that we live in. But it was not just our respiratory system that changed. Our minds changed as well. This is what it means to be "fallen." Hear me—mankind didn't fall in distance, he fell dimensionally. In other words, he fell mentally. Again, his spirit, which had once been in the front seat, was demoted and cast into the backseat, while his flesh, which had once been in the back seat, suddenly found itself in the driver's seat. So, man's soul (mind, will and emotions) also took a hit! Look at the chart below.

Man	Mankind
Led by the Spirit	Led by the flesh

The soul of a man follows whatever the man is being led by. If he's led by his flesh, his soul will be carnal; if he's led by his spirit, his soul will mind the things of God. Both men have different systems! A man led by his flesh has a different system than a man who's led by his spirit! This is why Apostle Paul told the Church at Rome (in Romans 12:2), "And be not conformed to this world: but be ye transformed by the renewing of your mind, that ye may prove what is that good, and acceptable, and perfect, will of God." He told the Church at Galatia, "This I say then, Walk in the Spirit, and ye shall not fulfill the lust of the flesh. For the flesh lusteth against the Spirit, and the Spirit against the flesh: and these are contrary the one to the other: so that ye cannot do the things that ye would. But if ye be led of the Spirit, ye are not under the law" (Galatians 5:16-18). The system of man is self-denial, but the system of mankind has to be managed by self-control. One is managed by the conscious; one is managed by the unconscious mind. Remember, the unconscious mind deals with stored memory and instinctual responses. The moment that Jesus died for our sins, another shift happened! All of a sudden, the spirit of mankind was catapulted back into its rightful position (for those who accept Him as their Messiah) and mankind's flesh was tossed into the backseat, but because of cellular memory (the theory that the body can and does house or remember trauma, much like the brain), the flesh of a man continued to pull him in the wrong direction. To counter this, God told us to "be transformed by the renewing of our minds." This simply means to stop breathing or functioning through the world's system. We can now breathe and function in Christ. It takes some time for a man who's been intoxicated and living in the dark to sober up enough to embrace the light, and this is why God gave us grace. Grace is the breathing tube that allows us to inhale the mercies of God while we're still in the wilderness of Sin (doubt, unbelief, perversion).

Remember, it's the green plants that provide us with the oxygen to live. What was found in the Garden of Eden? Plants, of course! What did God tell us to grow in our lives? The fruits of the Holy Spirit! Again, they are:

Love	Joy	Peace
Forbearance	Kindness	Goodness
Faithfulness	Gentleness	Self-Control

Again, man has a system, and mankind has his own system. Man functions on spiritual fruits, but mankind poisons himself with the works of the flesh. Both of these are two different systems that cannot coexist since one always cancels out the other (see the parable of the sower in Matthew 13). Why is this important for me to reiterate? Because anxiety is oftentimes the product or the chemical response of us attempting to man, manipulate or manage both systems! And of course, anxiety directly impacts our respiratory system, making it difficult for us to breathe. Anxiety is inflammation of the soul! Meditation is the tool that God designed to, not only relieve us, but to unclog our souls; this way, we can hear clearly what the Spirit of the Lord is saying to us.

- **Psalm 19:4:** Let the words of my mouth and the meditation of my heart be acceptable in your sight, O Lord, my rock and my redeemer.
- **Joshua 1:8:** This Book of the Law shall not depart from your mouth, but you shall meditate on it day and night, so that you may be careful to do according to all that is written in it. For then you will make your way prosperous, and then you will have good success.

Let's Breathe!

The following article was taken from the United States Department of Agriculture's website:

The Power of One Tree - The Very Air We Breathe

A tree has the ability to provide an essential of life for all living things on our planet – oxygen, and the power to remove harmful gases like carbon dioxide making the air we breathe healthier.

Here is how it works:

To keep it simple a tree is comprised of its leaves, stems, trunk and its roots. When you look at a tree, note that about five percent of the tree is comprised of its leaves, 15 percent its stems, 60 percent goes into its trunk and 20 percent is devoted to its roots.

Here is the superhero part. Through a process called photosynthesis, leaves pull in carbon dioxide and water and use the energy of the sun to convert this into chemical compounds such as sugars that feed the tree. But as a by-product of that chemical reaction oxygen is produced and released by the tree. It is proposed that one large tree can provide a day's supply of oxygen for up to four people.

Trees also store carbon dioxide in their fibers helping to clean the air and reduce the negative effects that this CO2 could have had on our environment. According to the Arbor Day Foundation, in one year a mature tree will absorb more than 48 pounds of carbon dioxide from the atmosphere and release oxygen in exchange. So next time you take a deep breath of air give credit to a tree or hug a tree in thanks for what it gives us – the very air we breathe.

Source: USDA.gov/The Power of One Tree - The Very Air We Breathe/Joanna Mounce Stancil, U.S. Forest Service

Mark 8:22-25 tells an all-too-familiar story. It reads, "And he cometh to Bethsaida; and they bring a blind man unto him, and besought him to touch him. And he took the blind man by the hand, and led him out of the town; and when he had spit on his eyes, and put his hands upon him, he asked him if he saw ought. And he looked up, and said, I see men as trees, walking. After that he put his hands again upon his eyes, and made him look up: and he was restored, and saw every man clearly." What can we take from this? It's simple. Trees are used to represent people. So, anytime you see wood in the scriptures, it's used to represent flesh. The same is true for dirt. Fruits, on the other hand, represent the manifestations of a man's heart and character. They aren't just acts or actions, fruits represent seeds, and seeds (of course) represent words. Everything that grows and begins to produce fruit in your life first started with a word or a set of words. If those words were received (accepted) by you or they weren't addressed (apathy), they eventually started to take root. What this means is, the words spoken over or into your life started growing anchors. In the world of botany, we call those anchors roots, and roots grow downward before a plant grows upward.

Inside of every seed, there is an embryo that is embedded in the plant's food supply (endosperm). Eventually, the embryo will split the covering or shell of the plant and the roots will anchor themselves in the ground. This stabilizes the plant, and allows it to absorb water and nutrients from the soil. Finally, the stem will begin to rise and break the soil, and the leaves will emerge from the shell. Eventually, the plant will reproduce after itself, but if there's no man to till the garden, a field or a forest will be born. If there is a man to till the land, however, a garden or a farm will be born. Of course, a garden is a place of order, whereas, forests and fields are places of chaos and disorder. Many, if not most, of the plants that grow in fields and forests found their way there through one of the three methods of seed dispersal:

Dispersal Type	Description	What This Means
Wind	Many of the seeds dropped by mature plants are carried away by the wind to a different location. Many of these seeds can travel miles, and if there's no man to manage the field that they fall in, they will produce a wilderness.	Of course, we know that winds represent words or doctrines. Many of the issues that can be found producing fruit in our lives are the products of what we've heard, what we've overheard, what we've been taught and what we've come to believe. This is why God initiated the five-fold ministry (see Ephesians 4:11-14).
Water	Many seeds fall into or are carried by the wind into small or large bodies of water, where they are carried away by the tide. Eventually, they will find their way to dry ground, where they will begin the germination process.	Water, in the scriptures, is used to symbolize many things, from baptism, purification, salvation, life and troublesome times. Obviously, seeds carried away by water represent seeds or beliefs that found their way into our lives during difficult seasons.
Animals	Some seeds are eaten by birds, but they are not fully digested. Instead, the chemicals found in the bird's digestive system only serves to weaken the seed's outer coat. The bird, of course, carries the	Birds, in this context, are used to represent demonic agents. Consider Abraham's sacrifice and how he had to keep the birds of prey from stealing his offering (see Genesis 15:11). Animals are also used to represent demonic

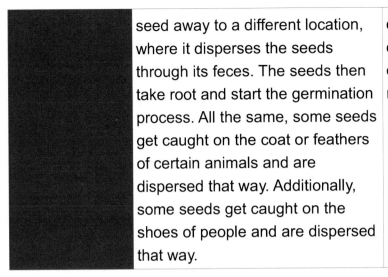

seed away to a different location, where it disperses the seeds through its feces. The seeds then take root and start the germination process. All the same, some seeds get caught on the coat or feathers of certain animals and are dispersed that way. Additionally, some seeds get caught on the shoes of people and are dispersed that way.	entities, so there are some seeds carried away (blessings) or brought into our lives (curses) that are the direct result of spiritual warfare.

It goes without saying that some seeds are good, while others are not-so-good. Then again, some seeds are good when they grow where they should grow, but they can be troublesome if they start growing in the wrong areas of a garden, for example. In the world of botany, farmers understand that there are some seeds that don't grow well together because of their chemical makeup. This is called plant incompatibility. Cabbage and cauliflower, for example, don't grow well together. Potatoes and tomatoes don't grow well together. Nevertheless, neither of these are bad vegetables; they all produce food, however, in a standard garden, you won't see them planted too close to one another. Now, let's revisit the Garden of Eden.

Genesis 2:7	Genesis 2:17	Genesis 3:4-5	Genesis 3:6	Genesis 3:22-23
And the LORD God formed man of the dust of the ground, and breathed into his nostrils the breath of life; and man became a living soul.	But of the tree of the knowledge of good and evil, thou shalt not eat of it: for in the day that thou eatest thereof thou shalt surely die.	And the serpent said unto the woman, Ye shall not surely die: For God doth know that in the day ye eat thereof, then your eyes shall be opened, and ye shall be as gods, knowing good and evil.	And when the woman saw that the tree was good for food, and that it was pleasant to the eyes, and a tree to be desired to make one wise, she took of the fruit thereof, and did eat, and gave also unto her husband with her; and he did eat.	And the LORD God said, Behold, the man is become as one of us, to know good and evil: and now, lest he put forth his hand, and take also of the tree of life, and eat, and live for ever: Therefore the LORD God sent him forth from the

				garden of Eden, to till the ground from whence he was taken.

Plant incompatibility. The blind man said, "I see men as trees." In the Garden, Adam saw many trees, all of which he had been given the commandment (and privilege) to tend to; that is, all except the Tree of the Knowledge of Good and Evil. The Garden was expansive; it was nothing like the small garden that we imagined it to be. The possibilities were endless. Adam and Eve could eat as much as they wanted to eat from any of the trees in the Garden except the Tree of the Knowledge of Good and Evil. But how had that tree gotten there? In truth, it served as a symbol of a fallen Lucifer. Remember, Lucifer had peered into the glory of God and saw something that he was supposed to cover! He saw the secrets or revelations of God; he saw the development and dominion of mankind! Lucifer also came across the expanse that we call darkness, and he realized (or thought) that this was uncharted territory. He had the knowledge of good (light) and evil (darkness), and he used that knowledge to deceive one third of God's angels. So, the fruits on the Tree of the Knowledge of Good and Evil all represented half-truths that Satan had sold or trafficked to the angels. When Eve bit into the fruit, it changed her very nature. Her digestive system had not been designed to filter out waste, so the waste had no way of escape except through her lips. In other words, Eve too became a liar. She made her way over to her husband and deceived him, and that's when his digestive system changed as well. With no exit to make its way to and through, the waste had to find its way out of Adam's lips as well. In other words, they became what they ate—liars! But wait, why hadn't God removed the Tree of the Knowledge of Good and Evil from His Garden? Why should He have to? The tree was symbolic of Lucifer's rise and fall. Remember, he and his angels had been cast into the Earth, but they had no bodies to inhabit, so Satan convinced a serpent to allow him to inhabit or borrow its body. Again, some seeds are dispersed through animals! Then again, some seeds are dispersed through humans (they get caught in our shoes). Satan spotted Eve and made his way over to her. From there, he began his deception. When Eve meditated on his lies, what she hadn't realized was that a seed had been planted in her heart, but it could only take root if she disobeyed God. She did just that, and from there, Satan had another body in which he could inhabit. The point is this—we need trees (people) to breathe; we need community! But we also need order! Without order, our life will become the equivalent of a field or a forest. Snakes love tall grass; snakes love to live in unmanned areas! Now, consider this—your soul is a garden or a forest. This, of course, depends entirely on what you've allowed to grow in your heart. This is why God told us to "guard our hearts." There are winds (words and doctrines) that our conscious minds are subjected to or immersed in every single day, and we must be diligent and ensuring that no demonic seeds find their way into our subconscious minds (hearts). Then again, the enemy will use any person he can use to hurt or injure us mentally and emotionally. This is when he'll use water (imaginations, temptations) to carry seeds into our lives. They can be thoughts of grandeur-based-revenge or violent thoughts. Either way, God told us to cast them down. In other words, heave them out! And lastly, there are seeds brought into our lives by demonic entities. They can be spirits that we're bound by, or spirits in the people we've surrounded ourselves with. Hear me—every bad seed that Satan tosses into your life is designed to counter a good seed! Remember, some plants don't grow well together! For example, fornication, which is a work or fruit of the flesh would counter long-suffering; the two cannot and will not grow together since one cancels out the other!

There are good trees (people) and good fruits (characteristics) growing in your life, but like the rest of us, you have some things growing that need to be uprooted because, hear me, not only will they produce fruit in your life, but the seeds from those fruits will carry over into the lives of those closest to or connected to you. We need trees to breathe, but there are some trees that cannot and should not grow in our gardens. The goal of meditation is to act as a wind, blowing away every lie that has made its way into our lives and has not yet taken root. Remember, winds come in varying forces or strengths, so anything that has taken root will require stronger winds. For example, light winds can blow away a seed, but it would take hurricane force winds to uproot and pull down a tree! This means that we have to root the Word so deep into our hearts until He begins to produce fruit in our lives; these fruits won't grow well with the other fruits that we are no longer watering.

Inhale. Exhale. Cast out the lies that are still sitting on the surface of your mind (conscious) and breathe in the Word of God. I love what Bible Study Tools had to say regarding the differences between biblical meditation versus the world's form of meditation. "Secular meditation is focused on letting go of our attachment to everything but the present moment, the present breath. Biblical meditation is focused on clinging as close as we can to the ways, promises and words of God" (Source: Bible Study Tools/What Does the Bible Say about Meditation?/Shelby Turner). How sound and true this is?! As believers, when we meditate, we do not do as the world does; we hold tight to the words of God until we can unite those words in our minds as the Word of God. We do not inhale possibilities because the Word of God is absolute; whatever we take in, we believe in, and we do not give way or opportunity to chance. Remember, the Greek word for "Genesis" means "origin." What is the genesis of your breath, meaning, where did it originate? Since we all know the answer to this question, let's move on to another question. Since God gave us the gift of life, how do we return, not just our souls to God, but our breaths? It's simple. We worship Him "in" spirit and in truth. How does this look?

We are three-dimensional; we've already established this, so worshiping God in spirit means to embed or engrave His Word within the innermost parts of us. It means to plant the Word in our hearts and allow the Tree of Life (Jesus) to grow through our soil (flesh) until people can only see Jesus when they look at us! This has everything to do with our beliefs; this means that our worship shouldn't just be surface-level (from the conscious mind), but it should be something we do instinctively (from the unconscious mind), meaning, it must be a part of our being. In other words, we don't just say the Word of God (any parakeet can mimic what it's heard), we believe the Word of God until we become a word of God. This means that God's Spirit should be so ingrained in our DNA that demons run from even our shadows. But how do we get to this level? It's simple. We meditate on the Word of God. This allows us to take the Word from our conscious to our subconscious.

What are the steps of meditation?
1. Find (or create) a quiet spot in your home, office, car or wherever you are. Remove anything that can or may serve as a distraction.
2. Sit in a comfortable position. Please note that you do NOT have to sit in the many meditation poses or forms that yoga practitioners use. Simply find a position that's comfortable for you, even if that's resting against a wall. (Note: you can also stand while you meditate. It's your choice!)
3. (Optional) Put on some music that calms you. Music is used in meditation to serve as a distraction from all the noise that our minds make.
4. Clear your mind. Don't think about your problems or anything else.
5. Start thinking about the love of God. Remember the victories you've had because of His love and His grace. Consider some of your favorite love stories in the Bible, for example, the story of God delivering His people from Egypt. Imagine the overwhelming love that they felt once they were on the other side of the Red Sea and Pharaoh was no longer a threat to them.
6. Quote the Word of God calmly. Be sure to break the Word down into smaller words so that you can digest Him. (And when he had given thanks, he brake it, and said, Take, eat: this is my body, which is broken for you: this do in remembrance of me.) You have to eat the Word in whatever portions that allow you to remember Him. For example, "The Lord is my Rock." Breathe in; breathe out. "The Lord is my fortress." Breathe in; breathe out. "The Lord is my deliverer." Breathe in; breathe out.

As you're meditating on Psalms 18:2 (for example), think about every time God acted in the many roles listed. Let's look at the scripture in its entirety. It reads, "The LORD is my rock, and my fortress, and my deliverer; my God, my strength, in whom I will trust; my buckler, and the horn of my salvation, and my high tower." Who is David identifying God as?

My Rock	My Fortress
My Deliverer	My God
My Strength (in whom I Trust)	My Buckler
Horn of My Salvation	My High Tower

So, as you can see, these are eight meditation points. Remember, every breakdown of a scripture or a sentence is a meditation point. For example, "In the beginning was the Word, and the Word was with God, and the Word was God. The same was in the beginning with God. All things were made by him; and without him was not any thing made that was made. In him was life; and the life was the light of men. And the light shineth in darkness; and the darkness comprehended it not." (John 1:1-5). This scripture can be broken down into many meditation points.

Meditation Points	
1	In the beginning.
2	In the Beginning was the Word.
3	The Word was with God.
4	The Word was God.
5	The same was in the beginning with God.
6	All things were made by Him.
7	Without Him was not anything made that was made.
8	In Him was life.
9	The Life was the light of men.
10	The light shined in the darkness.
11	The darkness comprehended it not.

Of course, you can break down this scripture (or every other scripture that you meditate on) in as many points as you can digest. Use your imagination to imagine God's glory covering every inch of your mind. As you breathe out, imagine all of the trash, debris, and ungodly seeds (lies) being blown out of your soul and escaping through your nose. Now inhale the Word of God. "For God so loved the world, that he gave his only begotten Son, that whosoever believeth in him should not perish, but have everlasting life" (John 3:16).

Meditation Points	
1	For God.
2	For God so loved.
3	For God so loved the world.
4	He gave His only begotten Son.
5	Whosoever believes in Him.
6	Whosoever believes in Him will not perish.
7	Whosoever believes in Him will not perish, but have everlasting life.
8	Whosoever believes in Him will have everlasting life.

Continue doing this until you are one with that scripture. Now, hear me—it has to graduate from being a scripture to being the Word of God; it has to graduate from being an "it" to a "Him." This process is called germination! This is the ultimate goal of meditation and reflection! Germination takes place when we experience the many facets, levels, and dimensions of God's love; this allows our vision to clear up until we stop seeing words and we learn to see the Word behind the words. Your goal is to plant the words in your mind, and God will send someone to water those words, and ultimately, He will bring the increase! As you read the scriptures, inhale the love of God and exhale every belief that is contrary to or serves to contradict what the Word says about Him and how He perceives you. Let's go back to sixth day of creation. Genesis 1:26-28 reads, "And God said, Let us make man in our image, after our likeness: and let them have dominion over the fish of the sea, and over the fowl of the air, and over the cattle, **and over all the earth**, and over every creeping thing that creepeth upon the earth. So God created man in his own image, in the image of God created he him; male and female created he them. And God blessed them, and God said unto them, Be fruitful, and multiply, and replenish the earth, and subdue it: and have dominion over the fish of the sea, and over the fowl of the air, and over every living thing that moveth upon the earth." What are you made of? The earth, of course! Hear me—dominion starts with you taming the wild beast that is your flesh; this includes your tongue! But again, meditation is a tool used to till or to dig the earth (your flesh). Why do farmers till the ground? According to Farmers.gov, "Farmers traditionally till to break up soil and prepare seedbeds." In other words, what we're doing when we meditate is we're plowing through our flesh and our conscious mind so that we can plant the Word in our subconscious, and allow Him to grow until He reaches our unconscious mind (the center of our breath or, better yet, spirit).

Breathe in. Imagine what Jesus did for us on the cross. Now, breathe out. Integrate your respiratory system with your imagination. Imagine every lie and every toxic thought that would try to demean or discredit what He did for you, and breathe it out. Root out the lies and allow in the Truth. This is how you create a garden. And remember, trees help you to breathe. In other words, the more good trees you plant in your garden, the more enhanced your life will be. Now reflect on the goodness, the mercies and the love of God. Continue doing this every day; this is what allows meditation to go from being a practice to a habit. Good habits weed out strongholds. Hear me—for the rest of your life, Satan is going to invite you into the darkness so he can lie to you and he can lie on you. But if you have an intimate relationship with God, you'll be like the two-thirds of God's angels who resisted and opposed him! You got this! Again, incorporate meditation and reflection in your day-to-day practices, and I am confident that you will see a major and noticeable change in your life! Happy breathing!

MEDITATION MOMENT

Be merciful unto me, O God, be merciful unto me: for my soul trusteth in thee: yea, in the shadow of thy wings will I make my refuge, until these calamities be overpast. I will cry unto God most high; unto God that performeth all things for me. He shall send from heaven, and save me from the reproach of him that would swallow me up. Selah. God shall send forth his mercy and his truth. My soul is among lions: and I lie even among them that are set on fire, even the sons of men, whose teeth are spears and arrows, and their tongue a sharp sword. Be thou exalted, O God, above the heavens; let thy glory be above all the earth. They have prepared a net for my steps; my soul is bowed down: they have digged a pit before me, into the midst whereof they are fallen themselves. Selah. My heart is fixed, O God, my heart is fixed: I will sing and give praise. Awake up, my glory; awake, psaltery and harp: I myself will awake early. I will praise thee, O Lord, among the people: I will sing unto thee among the nations. For thy mercy is great unto the heavens, and thy truth unto the clouds. Be thou exalted, O God, above the heavens: let thy glory be above all the earth.

What are the meditation points for you? List them below.

	Meditation Points
1	
2	
3	
4	
5	
6	
7	
8	
9	
10	
11	
12	
13	

WORD STUDY

List the words that stand out to you and conduct a word study.
Again, if you don't have space in this document, use another document.

Word	
Definition or Etymology	

Word	
Definition or Etymology	

Word	
Definition or Etymology	

LET'S REFLECT!

_____

_____

_____

_____

_____

_____

_____

_____

_____

_____

_____

_____

_____

MY ALARM CLOCK

Using the boxes below, record the dates when you had trouble sleeping.
Did you meditate that night? Write yes or no in the box provided.

Monday	Tuesday	Wednesday	Thursday	Friday	Saturday	Sunday

MEDITATIVE & REFLECTIVE TOOLS

Meditating on the Psalms of David

David's life was one riddled with joy, pain and many lessons that we all have benefited from, and regardless of the countless mistakes he made, God still referred to David as a man "after His own heart." This is why the book of Psalms is perfect for meditation. Below, you'll find a chart listing all of the Psalms of David, along with the probable timestamps of his journeys.

Psalms	After What Scripture	Probable Occasion on Which Each Psalm was Composed	B.C.
1	Neh 13:3	Written by David or Ezra, and placed as a preface to the Psalms	444
2	1Ch 17:27	On the delivery of the promise by Nathan to David-a prophecy of Christ's kingdom	1044
3	2Sa 15:29	On David's flight from Absalom	1023
4	2Sa 17:29	During the flight from Absalom	1023
5	2Sa 17:29	During the flight from Absalom	1023
6	1Ch 28:21	Inserted toward the end of David's life	1015
7	2Sa 16:14	On the reproaches of Shimei	1023
8	1Ch 28:21	Inserted toward the end of David's life	1015
9	1Sa 17:4, or 1Ch 16:43	On the victory over Goliath	1063
10	Dan 7:28	During the Babylonish captivity	539
11	1Sa 19:3	When David was advised to flee to the mountains	1062
12	1Ch 28:1	Inserted toward the end of David's life	1015
13, 14, 15	Dan 7:28	During the Babylonish captivity	539
16	1Ch 17:27, or 1Sa 27	On the delivery of the promise by Nathan to David	1044
17	1Sa 22:19	On the murder of the priests by Doeg	1060
18	2Sa 22:51	On the conclusion of David's wars	1019
19	1Ch 28:21	Inserted toward the end of David's life	1015
20, 21	2Sa 10:19	On the war with the Ammonites and Syrians	1036
22	1Ch 17:27	On the delivery of the promise by Nathan; or in sever	1044

		persecution	
23, 24	1Ch 28:21, or 1Ch 16:43	Inserted toward the end of David's life	1015
25, 26, 27	Dan 7:28	During the Babylonish captivity	539
28, 29	1Ch 28:21	Inserted toward the end of David's life	1015
30	1Ch 21:30	On the dedication of the threshing-floor of Araunah	1017
31	1Sa 23:12	On David's persecution by Saul	1060
32, 33	2Sa 12:15	On the pardon of David's adultery	1034
34	1Sa 21:15	On David's leaving the city of Gath	1060
35	1Sa 22:19	On David's persecution by Doeg	1060
36, 37	Dan 7:28	During the Babylonish captivity	539
38, 39, 40, 41	1Ch 28:21	Inserted toward the end of David's life	1015
42	2Sa 17:29	On David's flight from Absalom	1023
43	2Sa 17:29	On David's flight from Absalom	1023
44	2Ki 19:7	On the blasphemous message of Rabshekeh	710
45	1Ch 17:27	On the delivery of the promise by Nathan	1044
46	2Ch 20:26	On the victory of Jehoshaphat	896
47	2Ch 7:10	On the removal of the ark into the temple	1004
48	Ezr 6:22	On the dedication of the second temple	515
49, 50	Dan 7:28	During the Babylonish captivity	539
51	2Sa 12:15	Confession of David after his adultery	1034
52	1Sa 22:19	On David's persecution by Doeg	1060
53	Dan 7:28	During the Babylonish captivity	539
54	1Sa 23:23	On the treachery of the Ziphims to David	1060
55	2Sa 17:29	During the flight from Absalom	1023
56	1Sa 21:15	When David was with the Philistines in Gath	1060
57	1Sa 24:22	On David's refusal to kill Saul in the cave	1058
58	1Sa 24:22	Continuation of Ps. 57	1058

59	1Sa 19:17	On Saul surrounding the town of David	1061
60	1Ki 11:20	On the conquest of Edom by Joab	1040
61	1Ch 28:21	Inserted toward the end of David's life	1015
62	2Sa 17:29	In David's persecution by Absalom	1023
63	1Sa 24:22	Prayer of David in the wilderness of Engedi	1058
64	1Sa 22:19	On David's persecution by Saul	1060
65	1Ch 28:21	Inserted toward the end of David's life	1015
66	Ezr 3:13	On laying the foundation of the second temple	535
67	Dan 7:28	During the Babylonish captivity	539
68	2Sa 6:11	On the first removal of the ark	1045
69	1Ch 28:21	Inserted toward the end of David's life	1015
70, 71	2Sa 17:29	On Absalom's rebellion	1023
72	1Ch 29:19	On Solomon being made king by his father	1015
73	2Ki 19:19	On the destruction of Sennacherib	710
74	Jer 39:10	On the destruction of the city and temple	588
75, 76	2Ki 19:35	On the destruction of Sennacherib	710
77	Dan 7:28	During the Babylonish captivity	539
78	1Ch 28:21, or 2Ch 19:5, 6	Inserted toward the end of David's life	1015
79	Jer 39:10	On the destruction of the city and temple	588
80	Dan 7:28	During the Babylonish captivity	539
81	Ezr 6:22	On the dedication of the second temple	515
82	2Ch 19:7	On the appointment of judges by Jehoshaphat	897
83	Jer 39:10, or 2Ch 20	On the desolation caused by the Assyrians	588
84	Ezr 3:13	On the foundation of the second temple	535
85	Ezr 1:4	On the decree of Cyrus	536
86	1Ch 28:21	Inserted toward the end of David's life	1015
87	Ezr 3:7	On the return from the Babylonish captivity	536

88	Exd 2:25	During the affliction in Egypt	1531
89	Dan 7:28	During the Babylonish captivity	539
90	Num 14:45	On the shortening of man's life, etc.	1489
91	1Ch 28:10	After the advice of David to Solomon	1015
92, 93	Dan 7:28	During the Babylonish captivity	539
94	Jer 39:10	On the destruction of the city and temple	588
95	1Ch 28:21	Inserted toward the end of David's life	1015
96	1Ch 16:43	On the removal of the ark from Obed-edom's house	1051
97, 98, 99, 100	2Ch 7:10	On the removal of the ark into the temple	1004
101	1Ch 28:21	Inserted toward the end of David's life	1015
102	Dan 9:27	On the near termination of the captivity	538
103	2Sa 12:15	On the pardon of David's adultery	1034
104	1Ch 28:21	Inserted toward the end of David's life	1015
105, 106	1Ch 16:43	On the removal of the ark from Obed-edom's house	1051
107	Ezr 3:7	On the return from the captivity	536
108	1Ki 11:20	On the conquest of Edom by Joab	1040
109	1Sa 22:19	On David's persecution by Doeg	1060
110	1Ch 17:27	On the promise by Nathan to David	1044
111, 112, 113, 114	Ezr 3:7	On the return from the captivity	536
115	2Ch 20:26	On the victory of Jehoshaphat	896
116, 117	Ezr 3:7	On the return from the captivity	536
118	1Ch 17:27	On the promise by Nathan to David	1044
119	Neh 13:3	Manual of devotion by Ezra	444
120, 121, 122	1Ch 28:21	Inserted toward the end of David's life	1015
123	Dan 7:28	During the Babylonish captivity	539
124	1Ch 28:21	Inserted toward the end of David's life	1015
125	Ezr 3:7	On the return from the captivity	536

126	Ezr 1:4	On the decree of Cyrus	536
127, 128	Ezr 3:7	On the return from the captivity	536
129	Ezr 4:24	On the opposition of the Samaritans	535
130	Dan 7:28	During the Babylonish captivity	539
131	1Ch 28:21	Inserted toward the end of David's life	1015
132	1Ch 15:14	On the second removal of the ark	1051
133	1Ch 28:21	Inserted toward the end of David's life	1015
134	Ezr 3:7	On the return from the captivity	536
135, 136	2Ch 7:10	On the removal of the ark into the temple	1004
137	Dan 7:28	During the Babylonish captivity	539
138	Ezr 6:13	On the rebuilding of the temple	519
139	1Ch 13:4	Prayer of David when made king over all Israel	1048
140	1Sa 22:19	On David's persecution by Doeg	1060
141	1Sa 27:1	Prayer of David when driven from Judea	1055
142	1Sa 22:1	Prayer of David in the cave of Adullam	1060
143	2Sa 17:29	During the war with Absalom	1023
144	2Sa 17:29	On the victory over Absalom	1023
145	1Ch 28:10	David, when old, reviewing his past life	1015
146, 147, 148, 149, 150	Ezr 6:22	On the dedication of the second temple	515

Source: Blue Letter Bible

#	20 Facts About Breathing
	Breathing Facts
1	On average, we take around 20,000 breaths a day.
2	On average, we take around 8-16 breathes per minute.
3	We breathe in the equivalent of 13 pints of air every minute.
4	We inhale 20 percent oxygen, but exhale 15 percent of the oxygen we intake.
5	Seventy percent of the air we breathe is eliminated through our lungs as waste.
6	The lungs are the only organs that can float on water.
7	At rest, our bodies lose approximately 0.5 ounces of water every time we exhale.
8	Our right lungs are longer than our left lungs; this allows space for our hearts.
9	On average, women breathe slightly faster than men.
10	Our noses serve as filters, heaters and humidifiers.
11	People can hold their breaths twice as long underwater than they can do on land.
12	Most people only breathe through one nostril at a time.
13	The air we inhale is about 78 per cent nitrogen, 21 per cent oxygen, about 0.04 per cent carbon dioxide and one per cent other gases.
14	Our breathing is managed by our unconscious minds.
15	We can go up to 40 days without food, up to 3 days without water, but just 3-6 minutes without oxygen can cause irreversible brain damage, and after 15-20 minutes, recovery is virtually impossible.
16	Our cells need oxygen for aerobic respiration; this allows our bodies to extract energy from ingested foods.
17	If our lungs were laid out flat, they'd be the length of a tennis court!
18	The larynx (voice box) is located above the windpipe; it pushes air from the lungs through the voice box, thus converting it into sound.
19	Asthma, as well as many other lung problems, can be cured or improved by engaging in regular exercise.
20	Every time we yawn, our respiratory systems are responding to a lack of oxygen in our bodies.

Meditative Warfare

Below, you will find a list of common issues along with scriptures you can meditate on to address and uproot those issues.

Issue	Scriptures
Fear	2 Timothy 1:7; 2 Timothy 2:7; 1 John 4:18; Matthew 6:34; 1 Peter 5:6-7; Joshua 1:9; Isaiah 35:4; Isaiah 41:10; Psalm 27:1; Psalm 34:4; Psalm 56:3-4; Psalm 118:6; 1 Peter 3:14; Psalm 23:4; Psalm 56:3
Worry/Anxiety	Proverbs 12:25; John 14:1; Luke 12:22; Matthew 6:25-34; Psalm 94:19; Jeremiah 17:7-8; Philippians 4:6-7; Luke 12:24-34; John 14:27; Colossians 3:15; Psalms 55:22; 2 Thessalonians 3:16
Condemnation	Romans 8:1; Romans 8:34; John 3:7; John 8:11; 1 John 1:9; 1 John 3:20; Psalm 34:22; John 3:18; Romans 5:1-21; 2 Corinthians 5:17
Rejection	John 15:18; Psalm 27:10; Psalm 34:17-20; 1 Peter 2:4-5; Isaiah 53:3; John 1:11; Luke 10:16; Psalm 118:22; Isaiah 49:15; Deuteronomy 14:2
Persecution	Matthew 5:10-12; Matthew 5:44; John 15:18; 2 Timothy 3:12-13; 2 Corinthians 12:10; Luke 6:22; 1 John 3:13; Romans 8:35; Romans 12:14; John 15:20; 2 Corinthians 4:8-12; Mark 4:17; John 16:2
Abandonment	Psalm 27:10; Deuteronomy 31:8; Matthew 28:20; Isaiah 49:15-16; Hebrews 13:5-6; 1 Peter 5:6-7; Romans 8:35-39; 2 Corinthians 4:8-10
Sickness/Disease	Deuteronomy 32:39; Exodus 23:25; Isaiah 53:4-5; Jeremiah 17:14; Jeremiah 30:17; Jeremiah 33:6; 2 Chronicles 7:14-15; Isaiah 57:18-19
Sadness	Proverbs 12:25; Psalm 23:4; Psalm 34:18-19; Psalm 42:11; Psalm 55:22; Isaiah 53:4; Matthew 5:4; 2 Corinthians 1:3-4; Philippians 4:4-7
Poverty	2 Corinthians 8:9; Proverbs 24:33-34; Proverbs 28:6; Luke 6:20-21; Proverbs 21:5; Proverbs 15:16; Psalm 140:12; Isaiah 41:17; Matthew 11:24-25; Proverbs 31:20; Psalms 112-113; Psalm 14:6; Psalm 37:25
Death	John 3:16; John 11:26; Psalm 23:4; 2 Corinthians 5:6-8; John 14:1; John 16:22; Romans 8:18; Psalm 34:18; Psalm 147:3; Matthew 5:4; Ecclesiastes 3; Revelation 21:4; Romans 14:8; Luke 23:43; John 11:25-26; 1 Corinthians 15:26

My Meditative Measures (Journal)

Using the space below, list issues that you have dealt with or are currently dealing with.
Next, use your favorite search engine to find scriptures relating to those issues.
Be sure to record the scriptures below so that you can reference them whenever you need to.

Issue	
Scriptures	

Issue	
Scriptures	

Issue	
Scriptures	

Made in the USA
Columbia, SC
11 May 2021